HOW TO BE A

SUPER HERO

How to Recognize, Avoid, and Survive Violent Encounters, Assault, and Getting Shot in an Active Shooting

James R. Hiromasa

This book is dedicated to First Responders everywhere. Those are the every-day Super Heroes and deserve our respect and thanks. But whether by profession or by chance, anyone can be a super hero. Simply finding yourself in the right (or wrong) place at the right time and being able to do something about it makes you someone's, perhaps your own, first responder.

#dosomething

CONTENTS

"We don't rise to the level of our expectations, we fall to the level of our training." -- Archilochus, Greek lyrical poet

We live in an age of elevated violence, the kind where people are driven to take what they want from others simply because it's not fair that some people have things that others don't. Terrorists and mass shooters kill as many people as they can because they are different, and deranged individuals are led down a dangerous path of believing that if they are not accepted into a group then others should pay with their lives for not accepting them. With entitlement ideology at an all-time high and taking personal responsibility for one's action at an all-time low, it's no wonder crime against persons, assaults, random attacks, and flat-out violence against humanity is exploding.

The FBI's Uniform Crime Reporting Program shows that violent crime has risen for the second consecutive year in the U.S., and it's risen a lot. Overall, rape and aggravated assault both rose nearly 10% in two years, and murder rose a whopping 20%! Think about that number for a second — you are now 20% more likely to be murdered than you were just two years ago.

In 2016, there were 1.2 million violent crimes reported. In the FBI's UCR Program, violent crimes consist of murder, rape, robbery, and aggravated assault. Of the violent crimes reported to police in 2016, aggravated assault made up 64.3 percent, while robbery was 26.6 percent. Rape accounted for 7.7 percent of the violent crimes reported last year, and murder made up 1.4 percent.

On a positive note, property crimes are down significantly over the last two years, so there's that. Yet, we as individuals buy insurance in case our cars are stolen or wrecked, or our houses are destroyed, and we ensure our valuable belongings against theft, but why don't we as a society take these same steps to ensure safety against violence?

Why is personal safety lost on so many people? Mostly, it's because, on a subconscious level, people feel that it's completely out of their control. You can take steps to make your life safer in so many ways — safer cars, anti-slip devices, railings, helmets, warning signs — all under your control. But you *cannot* control what others choose to do to you; you don't get to pick the time, the method, or the person. It's like choosing to drive a car because of your fear of flying. Driving is one of the deadliest activities most people participate in freely and often, but no matter what happens, you still believe you can take control of the car to avoid a collision. That type of control just isn't possible on an airplane. We see the same false sense of confidence for personal safety — but with one deadly twist. The *vast* majority of people feel that they *will* be able to rise to the occasion, without any prior training or knowledge, to avoid "plane crash" assaults, random attacks, workplace violence, and mass murder incidents.

Here, you will uncover the secrets to stacking the odds in your favor and find the structure needed to build an entire safety plan — both for you personally and for others you influence or are under your care.

I NEEDED A SUPERHERO...and he showed up!

Imagine standing on a sidewalk, dressed up and out for the night, and there's a guy six feet in front of you with his right hand behind his back, telling you he's going to f**k you up. And he means it; you can see the handle of a kitchen knife sticking just into view. Do you know what you would do?

I don't have to imagine it, I've been there. After 16 years of accomplished martial arts training, I thought I'd know how to react, but as it turned out, I didn't. This was the night that I realized I'd been hiding behind a myth — that I would "rise to the occasion" if ever I needed to for real. But in reality, the Greek lyrical poet Archilochus had it right this whole time, *"We don't rise to the level of our expectations, we fall to the level of our training."*

In my 26 years up to that point, I had only been in a few schoolyard scuffles, and tossed a few drunks out of a nightclub, but I had never been faced with a sober, violent, possibly crazy person who would stab me just because he wanted to. I could perform some pretty amazing kicks and had some cool trophies, but none of that would help me here. I didn't even have a trophy handy to use as a bludgeon! I had no answers for this predicament that could cost me my life.

There I was, mind racing, staring at the knife handle doing the math — at six feet away, how long would I have to react once he lunged? Not enough time for the techniques racing through my head. Maybe I should launch a preemptive strike? It had better be the most effective I've ever thrown because I'm only going to get one shot at a surprise attack. And what if it doesn't work? What's my follow up if he starts stabbing me?

That's when it hit me: I knew I had to find a better way, a better answer, a *simpler* way. A way to not be psychologically terrorized by scumbags that are practiced in, and enjoy, violence. I never wanted to feel so helpless and fearful again.

Back then, looking for more and more complex techniques within a system or systems was the status quo, the dogmatic approach. What was needed was something *simpler* that could be accessed under fear and stress. Something that didn't require 1000 variations or fine motor skills — neither of which I had at the moment. I didn't need more complex training; I needed an entirely different approach! Weird how I thought of all that while waiting for this dude to come at me with a knife, huh?

Then and there I realized I needed to change my mindset, my training, my philosophy, and my psychology. That entire event could have been avoided all together if I had been more aware and more intuitive. And if not avoided, dealt with effectively had I had a plan.

That night was the start of my journey that would take me across the globe studying, learning, training, and studying even more. I observed acts of real, visceral violence while simultaneously learning how to stop it. What I found is that how most good civilians think of violence (defending against it, protecting from it, or avoiding it altogether) and how *real* violence is conducted are completely disconnected.

My goal is that this book will do several things for you: give you actionable information to be safer *now*, help you to choose the right type of class or training to learn to defend yourself, and get you to help drive others into action during times of crisis. Additionally, I sincerely hope that after reading this book, you have a better view of what real violence is and what it takes to stop it. I want this to inspire you to develop a plan for action and help educate others in your life to be proactive with their own safety.

So, how did my fateful night end? Well, I'm still here to write this book, and I avoided a stabbing. Not with skill, verbal judo, or fleet of foot — but by a shear stroke of luck. A superhero showed up just in the nick of time! He didn't fly in with a cape; he drove in with a badge. About 30 seconds into the standoff that felt like an hour, a police officer happened to drive down that deserted street and saw what looked like a conflict (boy, was it ever). He spun his car around and hit his lights, and the bad guy took off running. They caught him ditching the knife, and he did time for his crime. That officer was my superhero that day. And now I spend time helping make officers across the country safer in their daily contacts.

So how can you be your own superhero? Let's dig in! I'll guide you through it in three parts: Awareness, Avoidance, and Action. Think of this as your Triple-A violence insurance!

PART I

AWARENESS...SITUATIONAL AND OTHERWISE.

Intuition Awareness (Your gut feeling)

Have you ever gotten that feeling that something or someone just wasn't right? Right before something went wrong? It happens all the time, and there are real scientific reasons behind it. Malcolm Gladwell, author of Blink and Tipping Point, agrees: *"There can be as much value in the blink of an eye as in months of rational analysis."* And *"It would be interesting to find out what goes on in that moment when someone looks at you and comes to all sorts of conclusions."*

I remember one occasion when I was in Santa Monica, California, with a couple of friends exploring the 3rd Street promenade late one night. We had reached the north end and decided to jump up to 4th and make our way back south. Well, 4th Street is no 3rd Street, that's for sure. It's darker, with fewer shops open late and far fewer people. It gave me an uneasy feeling. We passed a parking garage and approached three steps between large pillars that led down to the storefronts, and I suddenly and quietly stopped my two compatriots. Something wasn't right. They looked at me like I was crazy, but I motioned that we should walk on the empty street, instead of the sidewalk, for a bit. I hadn't seen or heard anything. Maybe I smelled something, or maybe training told me this is a good ambush point. Whatever it was, I was right and likely avoided a problem. As we walked past, I saw a very large man in battered fatigues and long messy hair with a wicked menacing look on his face, staring us down. He was, in fact, positioned just out of sight behind a pillar at the top of the stairs, like he was hiding, not lounging. The sidewalk path would have taken us within two feet as we passed it, and we wouldn't have seen anyone until we passed — far too late to avoid an attack. There was no conflict, but I'm convinced it was because we took action based on my subconscious instinct.

This is why I stress the importance of being aware of, and trusting, your intuition. In danger versus survival, intuition isn't some wild, paranormal notion. The reasons your intuition kicks in aren't as important as your willingness to recognize and trust it. We are hardwired with certain senses that warn us of danger, and not all of those warnings are overt, particularly if we haven't experienced them before. A "red flag" coming from new stimulus or scenario may not seem like a warning, just a feeling, uneasiness, or perhaps even dreadful curiosity. You usually characterize it after the fact as a "gut feeling." The brain has a way of filling in unknown informational gaps with our own experiences, thereby altering the story altogether. Some of our red flags come from our DNA, where instincts were necessary for survival. Others come from our collection of memories and experiences, both real and imagined, remembered and forgotten, physical and mediated.

All of your instincts are derived from millennia of species survival all the way up through what you watched on YouTube this morning to draw conclusions almost instantaneously. It's only when we stop to analyze that we either second-guess these knee jerk reactions or we confirm them and take action. Gavin De Becker, author of The Gift Of Fear, put it nicely when he said intuition is always right in at least two important ways: It is always in response to something, and it always has your best interest at heart.

When you begin to pay attention to and are *aware* of your instinctive reactions, you'll start to understand what they are and learn to trust them. Only then will you be able to apply the next layers of the Triple A, Avoidance and Action, with purpose. These stages are when you can start putting plans into action instead of blindly reacting to a situation without control.

Situational Awareness (SA)

Remember the last time you bumped into someone or something while you were texting? Did you see the pictures of the guy who got hit by the bat in the stands at the baseball game? I hope that wasn't you — there have been a few. These experiences can be avoided by using what we industry nerds call situational awareness (often shortened to SA by the same nerds). Situational awareness is defined as "*the perception of the elements in the environment within a volume of time and space, comprehension of their meaning, and the projection of their status in the near future*" (Endsley, 1987, 1988).

Or, as I like to put it: *paying attention to what's going on around you.*

As a society, we are constantly buried in screens of one type or another. We pass what we consider unimportant time by entertaining ourselves or engaging with others via our devices. I challenge you to find any mass transit vehicle, waiting room, or lobby in America where the majority of the occupants are *not* on a smartphone. I don't necessarily condemn connectivity, but I do believe that *it kills your SA.*

Regardless of how good you think you are at multitasking, you're not. You're really switch tasking quickly. Our brains can really only focus on one thing at a time, a fact science has shown for years. (I'll let the good doctor explain it to you here.[1])

The good news is that things like walking, breathing, and eating are automatic, and therefore can be accomplished while you're doing other things, LIKE PAYING ATTENTION TO YOUR SURROUNDINGS, and picking up on body language, facial expressions, non-verbal familiarity between individuals, crowd movement, etc. Any of that ring a bell? Right now, you might be thinking about something that happened where some of these red flags were present. Are you? Take some time now to think about it. We'll cover some of the basics in a little bit.

---

[1] https://www.psychologytoday.com/blog/the-power-prime/201103/technology-myth-multitasking

But situational awareness isn't just about reading subtleties of human expression and interaction, although they're a fantastic study. SA is also about knowing your environment and yourself. Let's have a look at environmental awareness (not the conservationist kind).

For instance, it sounds cliché, but do you check to see where the exits are in restaurants and businesses? Knowing your way out and having a pre-loaded plan of action could save your life in an emergency. But simply knowing where the exits are isn't enough. In times of extreme stress and duress, your higher thought processes abandon you, and your survival instinct kicks in. The effects of stress on your cognitive thinking is dramatic and can be debilitating. We usually refer to it as "squirrel brain," when your processing ability mimics that of a squirrel crossing the road. You've seen it before — the squirrel is 90% of the way across and then sees you and it runs back to the safest place it knew — the other side. So like the squirrel, in a fire emergency or when explosions and gunshots go off, your brain screams, "GET OUT!" but doesn't tell you how. So you try to get out the only way your primitive brain knows — the same way you came in. This is one reason people die in house fires, because they attempt to escape the same way they have exited for years instead of going out a nearby window. (I'll expand on this more in the Avoidance section.)

A stark, grim, and sad reminder of people's problems with awareness is Rhode Island's 2003

Station Nightclub fire. Of the 462 in attendance, 100 perished and another 230 were injured. That means only 132 made it out alive and unharmed: less than 30%. Of the victims, 58 perished at or on their way to the front door (the one they entered from) even though it was not the closest exit for everyone, and even after it was completely cut off and blocked by crowds of people. Thirty-one of the victims were in the front door hallway, an area 6 ½ x 13 ½ feet, about the size of a bathroom. It's worth noting that although a member of the band on stage also perished, the others and their entourage escaped via the stage exit. You guessed it — the very door they used to enter and exit all day. It's safe to say their survival instincts also shrunk their cognitive ability, but it just so happens that their instinctive exit was less populated.

Another example of environmental situational awareness is going on the offensive. What in your immediate environment can you use to defend yourself from an attack? There are a lot of options in almost any environment, though some may take a little bit more imagination than others. An exercise I like to do in my live courses or presentations is to quickly identify objects in your immediate vicinity that you can re-purpose as a defensive tool or shield (sometimes referred to simply as "improvised weapons"). Take a moment now to look around you and identify five items within your reach. Now, take it a step further and imagine how you would use that object. How would you hold it? Can you swing it? A computer monitor (or keyboard) is often mentioned as a usable object in this exercise, but most people fail to realize that the video cable and/or power supply cable might very well anchor that monitor in place, or at the least severely limit its range of use — as anyone who's ever tried to remove a VGA cable that has been screwed in at the jack can attest! People propose lamps as well —same problem. If the power plug doesn't come out of the socket when you're swinging it, the lamp will be yanked right back out of your hand. Both of those objects can still be used, but you need a plan for them!

Being aware of your environment and the objects in it is an important step to forming your emergency plan. You really don't have to dedicate much time or effort to it, and you shouldn't let it take over your life. "Be prepared, not paranoid" is one of our mottos. Once you start practicing, it becomes second nature and takes almost no effort.

Behavioral Awareness

The ability to "read" people is a skill we are all born with. Unfortunately, our senses dull over time, and we quit paying close attention to signs that are less than overt. But our brains still receive and process these cues constantly, like how you feel when you first meet someone that creeps you out a bit. It can be hard to put your finger on why, but something just feels off. That's your brain telling you it sees something it doesn't like. These subtle mannerisms or micro expressions can go straight to your subconscious and put you on alert. Patrick Van Horne, author of Left of

Bang and CEO of the military training resource The CP Journal said that when a person feels threatened, scared, nervous, or begins to experience some other negative emotion, that person will display discomfort. Your life experience allows your subconscious to draw conclusions about those behaviors, which ultimately leads to uneasiness. What you do with that feeling or information is important.

One example of a time that a young woman got that uneasy feeling and, luckily, listened to her gut, which possibly saved her life, occurred during the summer of 2007. For safety reasons, I won't use her real name. I didn't know Jane then, but got to know her when she started training with us, and later worked for us as a fitness instructor. One day, we were discussing awareness and gut feelings, and the name Travis Forbes came up.

Who is Travis Forbes? Forbes is currently serving a life sentence plus 48 years for murdering 19-year-old Kenia Monge of Aurora, Colorado, a crime he confessed to while under arrest for assaulting Lydia Tillman. The assault included strangling her, dousing her with bleach, believing she was dead, and then setting fire to her apartment to cover his tracks. Lydia survived by jumping out of her second-story window, which left her in a coma for five weeks. Before these crimes, Forbes had a long history of criminal activity and assault.

Back in 2007, Jane worked directly with Forbes

for a while and then indirectly when Forbes continued working with Jane's company as a vendor. She vividly remembers the day she met him. Not because she knew what he did, but because of the way he made her feel. The moment they met and she shook his hand, she said she felt immediate trepidation. "The hairs on the back of my neck actually stood up," Jane told me. I asked her why. "I can't tell you exactly, but I remember he was trying so hard to be charming — it seemed like he was putting on a show. He was overly charming." Over 4 to 6 months of working together, Jane grew increasingly wary of being around him. She'd observe him angrily stomping around and throwing things when he thought he was alone, and then "do a complete flip, from extreme anger right back to overly charming when someone would walk in. It was eerie."

Later that year, Forbes physically placed himself between Jane and her office after closing and started up a conversation. She described it as normal conversation with a "you shall not pass" posture. It freaked her out to the point that she made it clear to her superiors that she would never work or close alone with Forbes again. Period.

Forbes eventually stopped doing business with Jane's company, and it wasn't until three years later that she heard his name again — this time on the news, and it sent shivers down her spine. She had known, innately and instinctively, that Forbes was dangerous and evil, without a good reason why. But Jane had a superpower — one that we all have — the difference is that she *listened* to hers, and it may have saved her life.

There wasn't much for Jane to see in Forbes that alerted her. But part of being a superhero sometimes requires you to stay alert for the more immediate, sometimes overt actions, behaviors, and mannerisms that should make you pay attention.[2] While I don't intend to provide you with an exhaustive list, my goal here is to alert you to two basic things to look for once your flags have been raised: 1) You need to have a baseline of someone's behavior before you can see changes, and 2) These red flags or behaviors are most urgent when they occur in clusters.

When someone is in a state of aggravation, fear, or stress, things happen to the body that it simply cannot control. Just like when someone is attacked or faced with an emergency, their "fight, flight, or freeze" (F3) system kicks in (causing squirrel brain), when a person experiences an aggravated or combative state, the body's fight or flight response system kicks in too. The same chemical dumps happen in both victim and attacker, the difference is just one's state of mind, and it will manifest itself in observable actions.

---

[2] Note, though, that this book is not a study in human psychology or a guide to body language and non-verbal communication. There are many resources from clinical experts, and I suggest you study as much of it as possible because once you learn what to look for and recognize, you can never un-learn it. You will begin see it everywhere! As a good friend and founder of the Core Body Language system put it to me like this: "Once you learn this stuff, you're going to see bad guys everywhere, and everyone you talk to is lying his ass off to you! You won't be able to turn it off!" And, don't use this on your wife...!

I'm sure you've experienced some of these yourself. How about sweaty palms? If you've ever been nervous in a big interview, presentation, or even on a date, your sweat glands may have taken over. How do you tell that someone has sweaty palms without being able to actually see them or feel them? Why, we rub them on our clothing of course! Rubbing the palms on your pants or even putting your hands in your pockets is a natural response. Because I talk a lot, my favorite is cotton mouth. Dry mouth is also a response to stress of one kind or another. How do you know someone has cotton mouth? They take a lot of small sips of water or seem to drink water in excess. My friends in the field call this "trauma water" and love giving suspects water to drink when they are interviewed about crime. As the questions circle closer to their involvement, they drink more water!

Next, let's look at clusters. An easy place to start is when someone is angry and arguing. This is easy to spot, we've all seen it and experienced it, but what is it we're seeing exactly? A very angry person usually displays several clusters of signals at once, which is why we instinctively know it's a dangerous place to be or approach. The most recognizable, and perhaps most noticeable, is elevated speech volume, which can be accompanied by changes in pitch as well. Our instincts to avoid danger are so finely tuned that we may be walking down a busy sidewalk deep in conversation with another person, but when you hear speech with these characteristics, you both stop and look. Add exaggerated arm movements, usually outward and upward (making oneself appear larger), widened eyes (taking in more information), and you have a cluster signaling that someone's subconscious is preparing for confrontation or combat.

This is what I mean by clusters. A person simply yelling or speaking loudly by itself doesn't tell us they're angry. Our brains need to see other indicators to put that flag up. Here are some other indicators you can look for:

Fidgety behavior: A person in a flight, fright, or freeze state may experience elevated adrenaline levels. Adrenaline is a powerful drug that makes you fast and strong. But once it's flowing, the body needs to use it somehow. Fidgeting and constant movement could be an indicator of increased adrenaline levels.

Flexing or wringing of the hands: In survival mode, the body sends more blood to the brain and core organs, stealing it from the extremities. With less blood flowing to the hands, the muscles get stiff, and the body needs to massage and stretch them to keep them working.

Stretching the back: This is a subconscious way of warming up. Just as we consciously warm up and stretch before sports or strenuous activity, the subconscious wants to do the same before combat or flight. It's a subtle gesture, until you see it, then you can't ever unsee it. Pushing the hip out to side, often with a hand placed on the hip, in an exaggerated fashion is one way it may manifest. Switching back and forth between hips is another way. If sped it up, it looks like someone stretching.

Bladed body: A person thinking about launching an attack may turn their strong side (right for right-handed people) away from you in a subconscious "wind up." Sometimes, you can see that part of their body being pulled away from you and then back toward you several times almost in a rhythmic swaying. Other times, it's static and loaded to their favored side. Baseline readings help here — is the individual left or right handed? Does the person always stand like that? Is there something else going on? The same posture may manifest in someone who is very uncomfortable interacting with you, and they will subconsciously turn their body partly away from you because they want to leave.

Target or exit glances: People may subconsciously look at the thing they want or are afraid of, or the direction they want to go. For a law enforcement officer, a suspect that glances often at the officer's gun should be afforded more space. Such a glance may be a subconscious signal of formulating a plan, and the brain wants to continuously locate the most important object of that plan. The suspect probably doesn't even notice it. The same can be true of someone who is looking to run, escape, or bolt past security. During conversation, people may even turn a full 180 degrees to make several glances at the exit before they take off running. It's pretty amazing to watch. When interviewed, they said they weren't even aware they were doing it!

Weapons check: If you see this, pay close attention. Sometimes people who carry concealed weapons will subconsciously and repeatedly touch the part of their bodies where weapons are concealed, particularly when they are getting ready to deploy their weapons. Gangbangers who wear large, loose shirts and carry weapons in their waistbands can often be seen pulling their shirts away from their bodies. This subconscious, and rather frequent, movement ensures the shape of the gun frame isn't printing through their clothing, thereby revealing that they are armed, it could be a motion that mimics the clearing of clothing to draw the weapon. And this doesn't just apply to criminals; even law-abiding citizens who carry concealed weapons may subconsciously touch or adjust clothing around the weapon. This happens so frequently, that in our firearms courses, we make a big deal out of it. We drive it home over and over again with a little humor so people remember, "Stop touching it! It's going to get infected!"

Grooming and self-soothing: This is a subtle, but important, indicator. Self-grooming and self-massaging are subconscious ways of calming oneself when agitated and not wanting to seem nervous. Stroking one's hair is a big one, as is rubbing the back of one's neck. Even you have made these gestures in times of stress. Other grooming indicators include: running your fingers over your real or imaginary mustache, touching the lips and corners of the mouth, clearing the corners of eyes, rubbing your forearms, fixing your clothing, and the list goes on. Without a baseline or clusters, these indicators don't allow you to make conclusions, but when observed together you may want to be on guard.

Using these practice routines, awareness exercises, and non-verbal communication behaviors, you can start to be more aware of the world around you. Without letting it consume your life, you can be better prepared for action if something does happen because you noticed it early and formulated a plan. Now, you can take *action*.

PART II

AVOIDANCE AND ESCAPE

A critical, and often overlooked, aspect of self-defense and self-protection is avoidance. Most trainers don't focus much on it because it's just not sexy. Learning to physically take down an active shooter is much more exciting in our imaginations and in advertisements than crossing the street to avoid something weird. Who's going to pay for that training? But here's the part no one talks about — good awareness and avoidance practices are responsible for saving exponentially more lives than all the physical applications of self-defense combined. The down side is that avoidance is not quantifiable. You simply cannot measure how many times something didn't happen.

What we can do, though, is look at instances where an attack or confrontation actually happened, and then backtrack to see where avoidance or escape were real possibilities. We can all think back to an uncomfortable or painful event in our own lives and trace our steps to see what we could have done differently using hindsight, which is almost always 20/20. But when doing this exercise, we must keep in mind that it's educational, and not beat ourselves up over opportunities missed.

We can also dissect other attacks or atrocities with which we don't have a personal connection, but in which an abundance of information exists. This is basically what police investigations do, particularly when an officer is attacked or killed. By tracing timelines, positions, locations, insight into attitudes and emotions, and many other factors, law enforcement can determine when, where, and how something happened and how it could have been avoided. In doing, they then develop training methods for other officers and new recruits based on what they learned, equipping newcomers the opportunity to avoid that same situation should they come upon it. The same exercises can be completed with information publicly available on the internet or through other public records.

Keep in mind that the "fire escape" examples throughout this book are, for the most part, interchangeable with "active shooter" escapes. That being said, let's circle back to the Station Nightclub fire mentioned in the Awareness section. We can learn from this and other disasters, and train ourselves to be more aware of alternate exits and routes of escape. As with any physical skill, you get better at it by practicing. But remember squirrel brain? Panic in the moment is going to negate 70% or more of your practice repetitions. So, if you walk to alternate exits two times when calm, under stress it's like you maybe did it once. Under extreme stress, it will lose the battle with the front door. This leads to a rule-of-three (the same rule we use when building our three-day emergency bags...but that's a different book!). The rule of three in this case says you should practice getting there a minimum of three times — for *each* exit. In the Station

Nightclub, there were four exits, not counting windows (see figure).

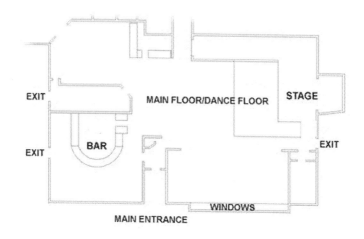

I know what you're thinking — that's not practical! And you're right. We have to balance our training and preparedness with practicality and reality. So in a concert hall that you're only in for one night, maybe you choose one alternate exit, and walk to it twice physically and 10 times mentally. Places like your work, home, school, and wherever else you spend time should be physically practiced over the course of a month or two. Of particular note should be exits that you can use at any time without activating alarms. If you have those, use them once a week in place of your normal exit. If that means taking the stairs instead of an elevator — bonus! You'll even get into better shape!

I had to do this on a practical basis. Years ago, my honor-roll daughter was selected to attend a meet-and-greet with Supreme Court Justice Sonia Sotomayor at the new Justice Center in Denver. At that time, tensions were high and people were highly divided. Threats to politicians were on the rise, and my wife and I were worried about the amount of exposure Justice Sotomayor's visit was garnering because she was scheduled to meet with a group of A+ students from high schools around the area.

Although my daughter was allowed to have a parent present, we were not permitted to be on the floor during the speech, Q&A, and subsequent meet-and-greet. Parents were relegated to the upper mezzanine balcony if they wanted to attend the event. I found this troubling because the event was held in the lobby of the newly constructed Justice Center (a potential domestic target in and of itself), covered by glass doors and windows, with only a single metal detector and a single state trooper on guard. Now mind you, I had faith in that trooper, and I made it a point to introduce myself to him and make enough small talk so that he would remember me in an emergency, but I wasn't worried about potential combat as much as I was about getting my kid out of there if something happened.

The front door through which we entered was behind everyone, and somewhat impeded by ropes and stanchions as well as the metal detector. Getting 100 people out of there fast would be a mess. So I located a back exit slightly off of a hallway behind the stage, walked there and checked it. Push bar, no alarm. Perfect. I poked my head outside — sidewalk, grass, trees, street, and cars. Perfect. I had my daughter accompany me to the door and, amidst much eye rolling, explained she was not to wait for me or use the front door in an emergency, but instead head out this door and across the open grass to the parked cars (cover and concealment) but to keep an eye on the door for me. I explained that if something sudden and violent happened (I should say reiterated, as she's heard it many times before) everyone would head to the front door without thinking. She would need to think, observe, and head to the back door if it's clear.

We walked back to the stage, and I pointed out where I'd be in the mezzanine and then walked with her back to the door under the premise that we should see if we'd have line of sight to each other from there. I walked the route three times myself, and my daughter practiced it twice. Good enough. Any more surely would have caught the attention of someone with good, solid situational awareness skills (we could only be so lucky). I asked her to repeat the plan mentally and then left her alone with her friends.

Of course, no emergency arose, she enjoyed her time, and networked well. But because we were prepared, I was less stressed about escape, which allowed me to focus and be more aware of others and the environment in the moment because we had a practiced plan. Don't get me wrong, this is not my normal level of engagement and readiness. This was a special case because I was there for one reason only — to keep my daughter safe in an emergency. I have no idea what Justice Sotomayor said to the kids that day. I was busy and, like I said, multitasking is a myth.

Here's another good example. I have a close family friend who is also a professional colleague, a top active SWAT firearms instructor and black-belt Krav Maga instructor, who sometimes joins me as an instructor in our courses abroad. He doesn't like flying much. He's sort of like Mr. T from the A-team: imposing presence, mohawk, hates airplanes — you get the picture (if you were born before 1980). When boarding a plane, he physically touches and counts every seat he passes between the nearest exit and his seat while walking down the aisle. Outwardly, I rib him every chance I get about it. But internally I've thought to myself, this is smart; if I can't see, or the emergency lights don't work, I may need to *feel* my way to the exit. And even more, it gives you a mental picture that allows you to run various scenarios. And because you've *touched* each seat, you've already done it, for real, at least once. Apply that to your office or classroom. How many desks or cubicles are in your way between you and the main or alternate exits? What else could get in your way?

Remember, extreme stress will make all of this 70% more difficult. But the more times you do it, the more memorable it will be in an emergency. I like to use the analogy of driving a car: When you were first learning to drive, driving in traffic or on the freeway was a very stressful event. White knuckled and physically exhausting. But after years of driving, you don't notice it at all. That's because practice, or training, can make you familiar enough with even a scary, life-altering or even deadly situation to make it less stressful. Driving can be a deadly activity, yet we rarely stress about it.

Think of some of your favorite action/spy/assassin movies. I'll bet more than one of them have a scene where one of the characters takes people out calmly, leaves, and orders a martini. Writers and directors like scenes like this because they charge us up emotionally and, at the same time, play to our ego because we would love to have such complete control. I like the way Bruce Siddle from the book, Sharpening the Warrior's Edge, puts it; "stress is a matter of perception and perceptions can be changed through the training process." Stress has real, physiological effects on our bodies. But those effects can be reduced — sometimes greatly — through training and experience.

When I'm giving a speech on self-defense or workplace violence, part of the homework I give the attendees is to physically practice a fire-escape drill in their homes with their kids at least once, preferably once a quarter, or even once a year. Practice the escape in full, including exiting through a window, using an escape ladder, or whatever the situation calls for, short of breaking out a window.

That reminds me, have you ever broken out a window before? Do you know how? What about a car window? You *can* try these things by visiting your local junkyard and buying a cheap door, or getting an extra home or apartment window for $5 at your re-purposed construction materials store. Although it has little to do with what most groups or companies hire me to speak about, the reasoning is solid. Practice it now, own it under stress. And if it can save a life or two, I'm okay with that.

Stress will mess with your body as well as your mind, by the way. Have you ever had a dream where you were being chased and could not run away without falling down? It's sort of like that. The adrenaline dump, combined with less blood-flow to the limbs, will reduce your ability to operate fine motor skills under stress. If you shake when you are scared, that's an effect of stress. Shaky hands after a particularly difficult workout is also an effect of stress.

We put some of our clients through some very simple tests while self-defense training to improve their stress-inoculation levels. In one test, we have the client strike a pad as hard and fast as he or she can for 30 seconds, then run across the room and grab a (deactivated) cell phone and punch in the numbers 911. Here's the kicker — the pad holder also gets to chase them to the phone while we count down loudly from five. Once we get to one, the pad holder gets to attack the client in some pre-determined way (safely, of course). You wouldn't believe the results. 911 is accurately dialed less than 30% of the time when first attempted. Extra numbers and wrong numbers were most common. After doing these types of drills a few times, the success rate increased dramatically, sometimes to 100%.

We use another type of drill that you might already be familiar with: finding a key, getting it in a keyhole, and unlocking a door while under stress. I'm sure you've experienced this. You may be able to do this perfectly on the first try when you're calm. Add stress and suddenly it's a Rubik's Cube.

These are both examples of how simple tasks that we take for granted can abandon us under stress. The higher the stress levels, or the more danger you're in, the worse your fine motor skills and coordination will be. The best way to overcome these deficiencies is to put yourself in these scenarios safely and train on them.

Now that you know the importance of practice, and its ability to improve your chances of escape under stress, let's get down to the skeletons of avoidance.

First, if you see a problem developing that causes your red flags to go up, just leave the area if at all possible. If you're walking down the street at night, and you see a group of guys standing along your chosen route, change your route. If you're in a group or at a gathering and something doesn't look or feel right, trust your instincts, gather your loved ones, and leave, or at least move them closer to an alternate exit. *I've done this a lot.* And you may have too. Ever been at a party where a group is starting to get too inebriated and loud? Maybe you felt a little uncomfortable. Maybe you left. Maybe you stuck around but luckily weren't involved in any melee that ensued. Or maybe you were. The bottom line is, if you can, avoid these things early and entirely.

Second, there are two buzz words that get tossed around a lot with regard to active shootings or other mass casualty attacks: cover and concealment. Understanding their differences and applications could be the difference between life and death. Concealment is relatively self-explanatory: It's any object that hides you from view. It is important to understand that's all it does. Hiding behind a bed sheet may conceal you, but it won't protect you. Concealment may also include standing behind a bright light or hiding in the shadows. Both are fine choices but offer no cover. One big misconception, largely perpetuated by television and movies, is about cover. Cover can sometimes be, and usually is, also concealment. But most concealment choices hardly ever offer any cover.

Cover is any object that will protect you from incoming fire. Important, right? But it's elusive. Think about your home for a moment. What do you think constitutes cover in your home? Unfortunately, almost nothing. The movies would have you believe that a refrigerator, a couch, or a bed offers good cover. Hardly. Walls? Not even. Doors? You wish. I've seen .22LR rounds penetrate two-inch, 150-pound solid wood doors easily.

A 9mm handgun round can easily cut through five full drywall walls and still have enough energy to penetrate at least nine inches into human flesh (measured with ballistics gel). That's 10 layers of drywall. How many places in your own home or office even have five full walls between areas in a straight line? That's like standing in a bedroom and firing a gun into the wall, and the bullet goes into and through bedroom #2, passing into the bathroom, through the far wall of that bathroom, into another bedroom #3, through that far wall into the kitchen, through the far kitchen wall into the foyer, and still penetrate an adult standing on the other side. Get the picture?

Modern appliances are made of millimeter-thin aluminum and foam insulation. Couches and chairs are light wood with foam and fabric. Office cubicles are paneling and foam, and elevator doors are thinner than those on a refrigerator. Your best bet for cover in your home or office is behind brick walls, or perhaps behind a steel column or a steel drum washing machine. The next best would be along the length of walls where a round would have to penetrate many layers of 2x4 studs. Door jambs, the framing in the walls around doors, for instance are usually stacked with at least two or three 2x4s. It's not great, but it's better than drywall. But don't mistake it for real, effective cover.

Consider this, if you're caught off guard with a shooter, and when you get squirrel brain, what are you most likely to do? Shrink and hide (or conceal). Wouldn't it be better if you'd considered, in advance, what could serve as cover? Maybe even set up a few things that *do* offer cover. It's not that expensive to get some ballistic material and build that into a cabinet, door, or tapestry. If you've planned in advance, your brain will help you out. If you didn't, you're at the mercy of the squirrel. This practice of "hardening" your classrooms, offices, or spaces in your home can be expensive. But some strategically placed bullet-resistant panels or fabric, along with a comprehensive barricade plan, can make a world of difference at a relatively low cost.

Let's look at a few specific locations now and discuss strategies for escaping, evading (avoidance), and even some barricading.

Schools, office buildings, homes

Earlier, when discussing practicing using alternate exits, I mentioned offices and navigating desks, cubicles, and taking the stairs. In an active attack or active shooter incident, you want to move, fast and with purpose, away from the noise and commotion. The adage "curiosity killed the cat" has stood the test of time for a reason. Your curiosity may want you to verify what's actually going on, but you have to fight that instinct. There is only one thing that sounds like gunfire in a closed space — gunfire in a closed space. If you hear it, leave. Stay low and move away from the sound to an alternate exit. Let me say emphatically here that I'm not a fan of the well-publicized mantra of barricading and sheltering in place, or lockdown, and we have the data to prove it. Being pro-active and running your survival program, regardless of outcome, will always produce far better chances than sitting and hoping. Hiding and hoping is not a plan, it's putting your life in the hands of the attacker. Doing something — anything —is always better.

The Virginia Tech shooting was a horrific event, a tragic and senseless loss of life at the hands of an evil person (I will never use mass murders' names; they don't deserve the press). We will never second-guess anyone's decisions in the moment because we weren't there. But what we can do is honor those who perished by analyzing the event and developing plans to save lives in the future.

In breaking down the testimony, investigations, and forensic evidence of the Virginia Tech shooting, we found that many, but not all, of the classrooms in the building went on traditional lockdown once the shooting started. After the initial stages, some rooms changed tactics. Our conclusion after studying this event and others is that *doing something works, doing nothing doesn't.* The data is available online if you want to break it down for yourself, but here's a very simple version that we researched and explains our conclusion:

The first classroom the shooter reached, Room 206, went into traditional lockdown. When it was over, 10 of the 14 people inside were killed; two others were wounded. In the adjacent Rooms 204, 205, 207 and 211, students and faculty temporarily barricaded or tried to barricade the doors. The results in each room:

- In Room 211, which also went into lockdown when shots were heard, 12 of 18 were killed, and six were wounded. (The room was initially barricaded by holding the door, but the shooter returned.)
- In Room 207, five of 13 were killed, (This room was also initially barricaded by holding the door, but the shooter returned.)
- In Room 204, 10 students jumped out of a window. Two of 19 were killed: the professor holding the door while others escaped, and one student. The professor was shot through the door.
- In Room 205, where a dozen students and faculty got on the ground and barricaded the door with their feet and a heavy table, preventing the shooter's entry, everyone survived.

What we see here is that taking action, as opposed to just hiding, had more of an effect on the shooter's ability to harm. Moreover, how you take action can make a difference as well.

Some students in 205 were wounded when the shooter shot through the door, as in room 204, but lying on the ground was incredibly smart. In our study of shootings that occurred through closed doors and walls, we found that the trajectories through those objects are all fairly similar: usually chest height and generally patterning no lower than 45 degrees from point of exit on the back of the wall to the secondary impact in the room. Usually far less than that.

The students in room 205 largely escaped injury because they were *close* to the shooter's position on the other side of the wall. If the students had barricaded the door and huddled on the *far side* of the room, they would likely have had many more injuries or fatalities (see figure).

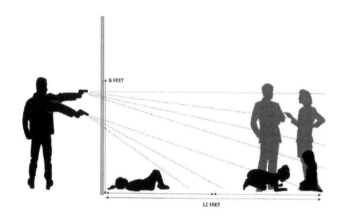

This is an important observation. We understand that barricading may end up being the best option at the moment, but it has to be done realistically, and with an alternative plan in mind. In other words, barricading should be a temporary solution planned in advance. It should be viewed as a method to buy time for escape or readiness for combating the situation; you can't barricade indefinitely as a defensive plan, and thus it should only be used as a temporary stop-gap measure. But it may be an important one. Just as the students in room 205 did, it should be considered wisely.

Barricades: Realistically speaking, we have to look at our environment and understand what would even constitute a barricade. As I discussed earlier, don't expect your barricading material to offer much, if any, cover. Heavy wooden tables or desks might help, but don't rely on them. It drives me crazy to see folks huddle kids together under desks or behind bookcases in classrooms, hiding from a shooter. This may sound callous, but why in the world would you put all the shooter's targets, in a 6 x 6 foot area? You are simply maximizing the shooter's ability to hit targets. At the very least, spread people out!

But I have an even better plan that that:

1. Your door needs to be solid. Not for cover but to withstand entry attempts. Standard home interior doors are not, so make a plan around that or change your doors. Newer office doors are generally heavier, but still do not constitute cover.

2. Barricade the door with heavy objects that take up little space. Depth is not your friend. The barricade's purpose is to stop the door from opening, not to provide cover — unless the barricade also has ballistic protection.

3. Three locking or blocking mechanisms, at varying heights on a door, is all it should take. Unless a shooter is intent on entering that room and that room only, and has a lot of time to devote to it, getting through a solid door with top, middle, and bottom locks is way too much

work, and they're likely to move on to easier targets.

4. Invest in some ballistic paneling or material. For instance, in classrooms if you install the material on the room's entry door wall from the ground up to 4 feet, you'd only need to buy 80 to 120 square feet of material. Run your drills to get the kids to lie down against that wall, and the ballistic protection, coupled with the likely angle of a shooter's trajectory, will do an effective job at a reasonable expenditure. The same goes for office buildings. Designate certain, strategically positioned, walls that have ballistic material installed behind them. You can create a "leap frog" exit plan that uses those areas for cover on the way to an emergency exit!

If you need help creating a plan or designing your own space, we're here to help. Contact us through www.wetrainsuperheros.com)

Businesses and restaurants

Your options are rather limited in these public spaces. Like your home or office, they usually have very little ballistic cover, but luckily, they are often built with or separated by brick or concrete walls. Of course, construction materials vary greatly by region, so you'll need to use your observation and awareness skills to determine that. By design, there is usually only one, sometimes two, public entrances to these types of facilities. Almost universally though, there are at least one or two other exits. You just need to know where to look.

Most standalone businesses have rear exits or delivery doors. Many cities' fire codes require a certain number of exits per square foot of public space. If not readily visible, look for exit signs above "employee only" backrooms. Again, building codes require the exit route be marked visible from the public areas. However don't count on it — code enforcement is rather lax.

Restaurants will usually have a back door through the kitchen. Unless you see staff taking deliveries and removing trash through the front doors, there's a back door. Like for businesses, look for an exit sign above the entrance to the kitchen. If you want to see for yourself, it's not hard to "get lost looking for the bathroom," and take a look around. I do it all the time; it's sort of a game to see who's going to question my being there first! Just say you're sorry, you were looking for a bathroom. If you're uncomfortable lying, tell the truth — you were looking for the emergency exit, just in case. That'll leave them thinking!

Streets, parks, outdoor spaces

The nice thing about these spaces is that there is usually an abundance of cover if you know what to look for. Some ideas for cover in these spaces include:

- Mature trees

- Low ground like ditches or hollows, or behind raised earth, like berms or hills.

- Corners of buildings

- Concrete trash receptacles, statues, or artwork pedestals

- Cars and other vehicles

Let's dissect the car in particular. Most of a car's body is made up of thin metal. A good hailstorm dents it, so it won't stop a bullet. The interior is mostly plastic, foam, and upholstery. However, the body's frame has more structure to it because it's designed to withstand collisions and rollovers. There are usually several vertical pillars, or posts on most cars that make up the vertical structure. The A and B pillars, on either side of the front windows, may offer more ballistic protection, but they are pretty narrow. The body of a car's doors may have some of this same structure material, but it too will be narrow. It's more like a cage than a box.

The engine block will offer a fair amount of cover, in fact the most cover the car has to offer. But it's not as big as it seems from the outside. Take a look under your hood to get an idea. Crouching behind the engine with your legs behind the wheel hubs will give you the engine, axle, wheel hubs, and break system as cover. Plus a little frame and drive train. That'll be your best position for cover behind a car.

Distance is also your friend. Depending on the nature of the attack, generally only a rifle or high explosive will be a real threat to you outside of 100 feet. At these distances, you will want to either keep moving, or find cover and keep watch to ensure that the danger isn't moving toward you. Like barricades, using cover in an active zone should be thought of as temporary. When you do utilize cover, make sure you have an avenue to escape to more cover or to put enough distance between you and the threat. In other words, don't seek cover at the end of a dead-end alley.

In this day and age, maximum civilian casualties are goals of terrorists and other perpetrators. These evil people have targeted, and will continue to target, large groups congregated in tight spaces. Some examples are malls, beaches, hotels, schools, nightclubs, concerts, and sporting events. These spaces are often described as "soft targets." Most of these venues check attendees for weapons, effectively disarming the crowd. Finding cover in when hundreds, thousands, or tens of thousands of people are also fleeing or seeking shelter is a daunting task, particularly in outdoor venues.

We most recently saw this on October 1, 2017 in Las Vegas. A man armed with a fully automatic rifle, or one modified to fire like one, fired into a crowd of 22,000 people from the 32nd floor of a neighboring hotel. Most people could not tell where the gunfire was coming from. Looking up for threats is not an instinctive response, and Las Vegas' echo chamber made it difficult to ascertain point of origin. The gunman was also some distance away, and we tend to look for threats that are much closer to us. The distance from the shooter to the crowd was approximately 1200 feet, or 400 yards. A decent marksman with minimal training can hit a single target at 400 yards with a scope and some time. Someone firing a fully automatic weapon, designed more for suppression of an enemy in battle as opposed to direct fire, will have almost no ability to target individuals from that distance, but spraying into a large crowd is an easier task.

In situations like these, do not go with the flow. Assuming that you can choose the direction you exit because it's outdoors, and unless cover is very close, break away from the crowds. A stationary shooter or shooters from 400 yards out with fully automatic weapon who wants to do maximum damage will shoot toward one place and one place only: the densest part of the crowd.

This is fairly counterintuitive because we tend to believe there is safety in numbers. However, what's really happening is your brain assumes someone knows where safety is because everyone is moving in one direction. Your brain also has calculated that out of 20,000 people, your chances of being hit in the crowd are low. Your brain is not your friend on this one, although it does have your best interests in mind. It's calculating the odds of you versus 20,000. It's better to remove yourself from the calculation altogether. Really, the situation will dictate whether or not that's the best strategy. But in Las Vegas, *if* you were aware of the distance to the shooter, the fact it was a fully automatic or similar weapon, and the difficult angle of firing from 300 feet up, it would be your best option. The chances that a shooter will blow through dozens of rounds of ammunition to single out one particular target in an open space are slim to none.

When you have to run through open space to avoid gunfire, run as fast as you can. It is hard enough to hit a moving target with a firearm under controlled training conditions, let alone doing it while under duress and the influence of adrenaline. So be the fastest moving target you can. Unless you're leap-frogging from cover to cover, utilizing cover or concealment as you move, the instinctive posture of making yourself small, bent over at the waist, with your knees bent, staying low, will slow you down dramatically.

Malls and other public places

I consider places like malls much like streets in terms of how they are laid out. If you walk through any mall, look in between some of the stores — almost all have a back network of hallways, or at least access to loading docks or delivery areas either through the interior of the business or in unmarked doors between stores. In some cases, bathrooms may be down a hallway. In any case, make an effort to locate these when you're browsing stores. Most places in the United States, if code compliant, have exit signs above storeroom access doors that lead outdoors. Many of these doors may be marked "Employee Only," but in an emergency, who cares. There is always a possibility that the actual exit doors may be blocked, that is unlikely in frequented and maintained public spaces.

One positive avoidance characteristic of malls and shopping centers is that they are almost always constructed of concrete and steel, which provide good corners for cover. However, interior walls between businesses may still only be aluminum studs and drywall, and cover may not help if you're in close proximity of a shooter. That's why awareness is so important and why taking action "left of bang" is so critical. "Left of bang" means before the bad stuff happens. That's where you want to be — alert, ready, prepared to respond to protect yourself and your loved ones" (Patrick Van Horne, Left of Bang: How the Marine Corps' Combat Hunter Program Can Save Your Life). Hopefully, you've noted suspicious behavior and moved yourself and others away from the immediate area already. If nothing happens, no harm no foul.

We've seen several mall shootings in recent history, and most of the casualties happen at or near the point of incident. As people begin to flee, choosing and engaging targets becomes more difficult for the attacker. One exception to this was the Nairobi Westgate Mall terrorist attack where four-to-six gunmen targeted an upscale mall in a murder spree that lasted for several hours, which was not fully cleared for three days. Sixty-seven people were reported killed and nearly 175 wounded. This is a stark reminder that *hiding in place is not a long-term survival plan.* After the initial shootings at Westgate, the terrorists actively searched for more victims they assumed (correctly) would be hiding in the mall. The best chance of survival came from immediately exiting the building.

Anywhere crowds gather could be a target for evil people. Nairobi is a world away, but don't forget the mass shootings at the Cascade Mall and the Tacoma Mall in separate incidents in Washington, the Westroads Mall in Nebraska, the Mall in Columbia, Maryland, and the many others here in the U.S. It happens everywhere.

And it's not just malls; theaters can also be tricky places. The nature of the design of most modern theaters are such that nearly all exits are located at the front of the auditorium, with only two or three walkways that feed those exits. As we saw in another notorious attack at an Aurora, Colorado theater, a shooter up front can do a lot of damage as people scramble to get past him to the exits. Theater seats are plastic and foam, offering possible concealment but certainly no cover. Staying low and using interior short walls or seating to stay out of sight *while moving* is important here. It's likely the shooter is looking to inflict maximum victim count and damage as opposed to spraying into chairs, so here you want to stay low and move.

Aside from that, there's not much else you can do, except position yourself close to an exit to begin with, which are usually the front-row seats that make it hard to see the screen or about one-third to half of the way in. The problem is that it's a coin toss as to which exit the assaulting party will enter or station near. Some theaters have a short wall or railing that borders the entrance walkway and the stairs. It's always possible that you can jump, climb over this, and drop down to the exit hall, but you'll need to look at your theater's layout in advance. Such limited exits cause choke points, known as "fatal funnels" that draw fire to them. In some cases, you may want to think about engaging the shooter as opposed to getting stuck in a fatal funnel. More on that now.

PART III

ACTION

While we devote a great deal of time and effort to educating the public and private sectors about awareness and avoidance, when it comes down to it, teaching people how to take action is where we live. This is one of the ways our seminars are unique: they balance awareness education with active avoidance strategies and the physical training necessary to confront violence or even take down a mass murderer.

This is the hardest part of my job. Not the physical training, but convincing people that they need to train and practice! I wish I could simply give a talk or write a book and make people better at physically defending against violence, but that's a pipe dream. We humans simply cannot excel at physical performance without practice. And here's the worst part — the bad guys *are* practiced at violence. Chances are they've done this before, and often. They're comfortable with the physicality of violence.

There is hardly anything I'm more passionate about in my professional career than trying to reverse the "one and done" mentality when it comes to self-defense training. If you want to beat Tiger Woods at golf, taking a golf seminar isn't going to do it for you. Heck, it doesn't even have to be Tiger — if you haven't golfed often, beating *me* at golf would require more than a single seminar, and couldn't even win an amateur golf tournament (I shoot a respectable 80-85, with a few mulligans).

There is no other physical activity or sport where people believe that a single seminar is enough to get by. Sure, depending on whom you learn from and what you're learning, you may pick up something valuable that works in your time of need, but should you come across someone that's practiced at violence, you'll probably need more.

How did this misperception about self-defense begin? Well, it started in the martial arts. Back in the day, and unfortunately still today to some degree, martial arts "masters" enveloped their art in mysticism — mostly for business reasons. These same masters realized that if the public believed they had secret techniques that could kill or disable an attacker with one blow, the public would pay to learn it. And if the technique looked esoteric enough, and given that 99.99% of the public who paid for it would never be in a position to have to try to apply it, they could tell them it worked and sell it over and over. Regardless of whether you believe in the secret "Dim-Mak" death touch, this marketing device mislead the general public on how martial arts and self-defense really worked.

I'm happy to say that today there are many more honest martial arts schools out there than even 10 years ago, and the general public is slowly catching on to those who still try to sell snake oil, largely thanks to the popularity of MMA and the UFC. But the myth that a single one-hour seminar on self-defense is enough persists. There is much more to be said on this subject, and I delve much deeper into it in another book I'm writing currently called The Training Crucible — look for it in 2018.

With that, keep in mind that the techniques I discuss here will yield the best results, even against seasoned violence, if you practice somewhat regularly. Any training is better than no training, but more training is better than a single training. Just like the saying goes in outdoor survival: Two is one and one is none[3]. Now that you understand what it takes to be able to take some trained action, and now that you've been made aware of your surroundings and others' behaviors, let's dig into it.

So, if you're aware of your surroundings and you're aware of others' behaviors, and you see a problem, what do you do? Take action! That doesn't mean running in, guns blazing, or punching someone in the face (although I bet some of you just imagined that and felt pretty satisfied at the thought!) Taking action requires measuring your actions and responding accordingly.

---

[3] For instance, when it comes to making fire, having two fire-starting devices means you will still have one if something happens to the other one, like it gets wet. In cave exploration, for example, it's suggested you have no less than three independent light sources, because you will inevitably drop one, break one, or one will malfunction. In caving, losing light means losing life.

Remember the Triple A of violence: Awareness (check), now you need to choose between Avoidance (preferable if possible), and Action (which may include avoidance at first). Taking action could range from just keeping an eye on something to trying to physically stop an attack yourself. Action can be as simple as crossing the street or changing your route to avoid a group of people that make you uncomfortable. Or it could mean calling 911 and letting professionals figure it out. You'd be surprised how often these simple actions aren't taken when they should be. People now seem reluctant to call 911, but police are, 90% of the time, a reactive force. They respond to crimes and discover what happened. I know they would all much rather serve as a *preventative* force. But they can't prevent a crime if they aren't aware it's happening.

In fact, I was out East working on this very section of the book when one morning I received a note from one of our trainees in Colorado who heard a woman screaming, "Stop!" in a horrid tone the night before (we talked about vocal tone earlier, remember?) He immediately called 911 and notified them of the location, the nature of the emergency and his own description, then grabbed a baseball bat and his pistol and made his way out to investigate the situation and help if he could. He came upon a group of six or seven men surrounding a woman who he couldn't quite make out. It turned out they were relatives and friends comforting her about the recent loss of her brother, and her cries and screams were in anguish, not fear. Once he discovered this, our trainee immediately called dispatch back and waived them off, explaining the situation. But this is an example of taking action. We feel that everyone should take the responsibility to call 911 in these types of situations. Arming yourself and rushing into an unknown situation is a personal choice, and frankly I'm proud to be associated with a guy who would do so. This bystander admitted afterwards he was "shaking and mildly sick, knowing that I am prepared to both kill and die for someone that I have never met, or even seen." Definition: superhero.

Taking action is one thing, but choosing which action to take is another. Here's an example about calling for help, and why under stress, your first action may not be as helpful as you'd like to think. This comes from another one of my talks and training sessions I did for a law firm a while back. While the details of the case are a little hazy to me (it was some time ago), the gist of this story is not only true, but common. While gathering intel from the company to prepare my presentation, I asked if there were any past incidents at the office that may have sparked the interest in my course. One person recounted an incident of an ex-husband who came into the firm that was representing his ex-wife in the divorce. He asked to speak to the attorney assigned to her case. At first, he was cordial (but there were clusters of red flags), but after he was told that the attorney wasn't in, and the receptionist couldn't divulge when he'd be back, he became more and more agitated. The receptionist even asked him to leave at one point, but he refused. He demanded to speak to the boss and wouldn't leave without doing so. She then picked up the phone and called her boss. Not 911, but her boss who was out of town on vacation. This is unfortunately typical. There are times our own kids call us in a situation, and we tell them to hang up and call the police. When in fear, you go to your last known safe place or the person who solves all your problems. If you're a kid, that's your parents; if you're at work, that's your boss. Why the boss? Because the boss handles all the problems at the office, every day. He or she will know what to do, right? This story has a happy enough ending. When the receptionist gave the phone to the irate ex, the boss was able to talk him down. It didn't go badly, but it sure could have.

Decisive, explosive action

I'm sorry to be the one to break this to you, but you were likely lied to when you were growing up. Time and time again our teachers, maybe our parents, and other people in trusted positions helping raise us told us, "Violence doesn't solve anything." Well, I'm here to tell you that it does. In particular, violence solves the problem of violence. The only thing that stops violence in action is more violence. It would be great that if while someone was trying to kill us, we could get them to talk about their feelings and hug it out, but that's just not going to happen. Might that happen before or after an altercation? You bet! And I hope it does. But *during* the act, you must be comfortable with violence to stop it.

Now it's come to a point when you can no longer barricade, avoid, or escape. Either by choice, fate, or a lack of options, you have to confront this violence face-to-face, head on, with whatever you have at your disposal.

Here's where I'd be remiss not to advocate for arming yourself. This book is not about carrying a gun and all the responsibilities that come with it, but the best way to stop violence immediately is with more violence, period. You've heard, "Don't bring a knife to a gunfight" and similar clichés. If you have to confront a shooter, you're going to wish you and about 20 of your friends had firearms. If you want to know more about the training and responsibilities of being armed, check out my books, The Modern Gunfighter (2018) and The Training Crucible (2018).

But being armed doesn't necessarily mean carrying a gun. You can arm yourself with an object in your environment, as I discussed in the awareness section. And remember, it's also not just about mass casualty events; you could be on the street in Kailua Oahu, which is where I confronted my potential attacker with a knife. Because personal attacks are quite different from mass casualty events, I'm going to break down how to take action into two categories: self-defense and third-party defense. Third-party defense is simply defined here as defending anyone but yourself from an imminent or active attack.

First, self-defense. We define self-defense in our Krav Maga training centers and seminars as "defending against an attack that is imminent or has already begun." We don't characterize this type of action as "fighting" because that word has different connotations. However, self-defense can and will usually turn into something that requires some fighting skills. Allow me to explain.

One of the overriding principles of the self-defense system Krav Maga is that it is intended to defend against an immediate threat and counterattack simultaneously. Imagine someone has a gun pointed at your head. This would be a bad time to kick the person in the groin, wouldn't it? However, you can defend yourself by moving and controlling the line of fire of the gun, and that enables you to strike the gunman in a moment of relative safety. Make sense? Here's a less dramatic, but very common, example. Someone has you in an arm choke from behind, and it's deep; depending on your personal body type and physiology, you might have anywhere from 5 to 15 seconds before you pass out. You could start trying to strike your attacker, but strikes behind you at this range are unlikely to be very effective. And while you're trying to strike, the clock is ticking. So instead, you should deal with the choke first. Strike simultaneously if possible, but the choke is your highest priority.

That being said, we highly value that simultaneous strike. Champion boxer Mike Tyson once said, "Everyone has a plan until they get punched in the face." And it's so true. True enough that when we're presented with two choices for a solution to defend an attack, and it doesn't violate any of our principles, we'll default to the one that allows for a simultaneous counterattack even if the other technique may be slightly better.

When someone has a plan of attack, you not only want to defend yourself but also disrupt the plan. You want to make the attacker change angles, positions, and balance — anything and everything you can to disrupt the plan will be to your benefit. By delivering a strong simultaneous counterattack to during your initial defense, you can turn the tables on the mental and physical interaction between you and the attacker, allowing you to go on the offense while putting the attacker on defense!

Here's the example I use all the time in my talks: A stabbing victim is not usually stabbed only once. Stabbing someone is a violent personal attack that is normally delivered repeatedly at high speed. Just look up "stabbing victims" and "number of stab wounds." You'll generally find dozens or more wounds per incident. Attackers turn into human sewing machines when they stab other humans. It's short, fast, and repetitive. So you can imagine that attacker has a plan to stab you repeatedly. If you block the first stab, then what? The attacker's arm will already be recoiled and delivering another stab, probably at another angle such that you have to be both *reactive* and *correct* again and again. But instead, try this: When you block (or attempt to block) the first stab, you can simultaneously punch then in the face as hard as you can. By doing this, you're giving yourself the best chance at disrupting the ongoing attack, perhaps giving you enough time to control the stabbing arm, get away, or arm yourself.

Some professionals refer to this as disrupting or re-setting the attacker's OODA loop. OODA stands for Observe, Orient, Decide, and Act. Ostensibly, it's our brain's computer program for any given activity. The attacker observes the victim, orientates himself to a position, decides to act, and then acts. Likewise, the attacker observes his fist stab was blocked, but he's already orientated to a position to recoil and stab again and has already made the decision to act. When the attacker is punched, it re-sets the OODA process because what he thought was going to happen changed and he now must adapt. Get it?

The alternative is not pretty, trust me. I have two training videos that I use, often side-by-side, in my presentations. One is of a stabbing in a bar caught on security cameras, the other is an almost identical situation in a convenience store with punches instead of stabbing, though you'd never know the difference until it was too late. I'll spare you the details, but what are important are the reactions of the victims and their outcomes. In the bar, the victim tried back peddling while flailing with his arms to stop the attack. As a result, he sustained 44 wounds in about 14 seconds (some of which were defensive wounds from single stabs on his hands and arms, hence the three-wounds per second average). The attacker's plan went undisrupted for 14 seconds.

In the convenience store, a very similar situation unfolds, with almost identical posture and proximity as in the bar, but this time when the attacker throws his punch (which looked exactly like the first stab to the neck in the bar), his intended victim was able to get his arm up in time to block the punch but more impressively, launched a nearly simultaneous counter-punch to the attacker's face. The punch caught him so off guard that the defender then was able to throw several more punches, ultimately knocking the attacker unconscious on the floor! All in about 1.5 seconds. See my point?

One of our guiding principles is worth repeating: Your plan should be to defend yourself from the immediate threat, launch a counterattack, and not stop until you're safe. Let's visit more important principles of self-defense.

Principles of self-defense

As I discussed in the very beginning of this book, more techniques do not always equate to better defense. In fact, they often have the opposite effect of slowing down your brain to decide which to use. It's based on Hick's Law[4], which argues that the time it takes a person to make a decision logarithmically expands based on the number of choices available. In the case of self-defense, this can be deadly. Imagine trying to decide on the best technique to defend that knife stab in $1/10^{th}$ of a second based on how the attacker is holding the knife, which hand the weapon is in, and other environmental factors. Too late, you've already been stabbed three times. So, we recognize that less is more when it comes to self-defense.

For that reason, we attempt to instill principles into our trainees instead of just techniques during physical self-defense training. This allows us to teach a single defense that can be effective against many variations of the attack.

Here are the framework principles we use:

- Deal with the immediate threat first.

---

[4] The proposition that choice reaction time increases as the logarithm of the number of alternatives. The law is usually expressed by the formula $RT = a + b \log_2 (n + 1)$, where a and b are constants representing the intercept and slope of the function, respectively, and n is the number of alternatives. (OxfordReference.com)

- Counterattack simultaneously or immediately after.
- Continue counterattacks relentlessly until safe.
- A technique's initial movement should be as close to instinct as possible, thereby reducing the learning curve significantly.
- Techniques should be broad, gross motor movements and explosive. (We already discussed the problem with fine motor skills earlier.)
- Never give up one position for a worse one (for example, don't turn your back even to deliver a cool spinning kick technique).
- Always "give" something when moving (strike while moving or changing your position).

We also have additional principles for more specific types of attacks, such as threats with firearms. The above principles are global, so they apply here too. Firearms defense principles, *in order,* are:

- Redirect the line of fire using the least detectable movement.
- Control the weapon and line of fire after redirection.
- Simultaneously counterattack.
- Disarm or secure more leveraged control while continuing to counterattack until the gunman is no longer a threat or you can disarm.

You can see how these more specific principles correspond with those in the global framework. That helps people learn quickly and retain the information over longer periods of time.

Practical applications

Before I discuss defending other people, I'd like you to have some practical working examples of exactly *how* to deal with a few common attacks. The actual skills you'll use to defend yourself will help when defending others as well. This book is, by no means, a complete training manual and even extensive manuals on self-defense really won't do you much good without 1) an experienced training partner and 2) a coach or instructor to provide feedback. Learning self-defense and fighting from a book is akin to learning to swim in sand. With that, the following offers some technical explanations and practical applications that range from basic to more advanced, and eventually, extremely high risk. *Do not attempt any of these defenses, particularly the weapons defenses, with real or replica weapons without a trained professional on hand.* In addition, practicing the strikes without proper protection can lead to injury or death. If you ever have any questions on these techniques, reach out to us at www.wetrainsuperheros.com.

Striking

It's important to note here that I will not be discussing fighting in the terms of sanctioned matches of any kind. Although defending yourself is immensely helpful in "fights," training for the ring or cage fighting is quite different than the training for self-defense, even though the techniques are much the same. So, when I discuss strikes, I intend that you use every ounce of destructive power you can manage behind every single strike. You're not in it for the long haul; there are no rounds, and there is no referee. Your goal is to finish quickly and end the problem or escape.

Don't get me wrong, fight training will advance your skills by light years. But as a trainer for self-defense, I must start with the assumption that you will not dedicate at least six hours a week to fight training, and that shouldn't preclude you from learning to defend yourself! Just understand that you will be *better* if you do learn the art of fighting. In a prolonged engagement, it will improve your chances of survival dramatically.

On the other hand, you can't "fight" someone when there is a gun to your head or someone trying to stab you. In these situations, you have to *defend* yourself and destroy the attacker's ability to continue attacking. That's different than a fight. Here there are no rules, and you must think outside the box and "cheat" as much as possible. Take every advantage you can.

I have a little pep talk I give at almost every physical training seminar I teach. The short version goes something like this: When striking another human being, it is both impractical and immoral to hit them with *less* than everything you have. Holding back, or hitting them a little bit, means that you were not in serious fear for your life, your safety, or someone else's. So, if you have to hit someone but don't want to hit hard, you should probably just walk away. The same goes with shooting someone. You shoot to stop someone who is causing you imminent fear for your life or may cause you, or someone else, great bodily harm. That means you shoot center mass repeatedly until the threat has stopped. "Aiming for the legs" is not only almost entirely impossible (stress, squirrel brain, movement dynamics, etc.), but it also means you were not really in fear for your life. If you had the wherewithal to actually aim for and shoot the legs, with little guarantee that it would stop an attacker, then you weren't in enough trouble as to convince anyone that you feared for your life.

The moral here is to deliver strikes with the most force you can possibly muster and end the altercation as quickly as possible. How do you do that? You hit with the proper tool, you target the right area, and you use your body to sponsor every single strike. Here's how:

Whenever we teach striking in our courses or seminars, we structure the lesson using the acronym WTF to make digesting and retaining the information easier. You are probably familiar with WTF as the generational shorthand for "What The F*ck." That's why it's easy to remember. Here though, it stands for Weapon, Target, Function. Weapon: What part of the body are you hitting with. Target: What are you aiming for on the attacker's body. Function: What you do with your body to deploy the strike effectively.

A word about targeting: You'd be amazed at how much punishment the human body can take. There are really only three ways to immediately stop a human from carrying on an action or advancing: shut down the brain, sever the spine, or break down the structure. The first two are self-explanatory. Breaking down the structure means destroying the bones that hold up the body or operate the part you're trying to stop. In firearms training, for instance, we talk about an attacker running at you with a weapon, like a knife. If you want to stop the attacker by breaking down his or her structure, you'll likely want to shoot to destroy the bones in the hips, most likely.[5] When striking another person, your best bet is to hit the face near the jaw, trying to get the head to sharply snap or rotate, hopefully causing dizziness or unconsciousness.

Personal impact weapons:

Our go-to instinctive weapons are the same as our instinctive defensive options: our hands. The three most common ways to strike with the hands are punches, hammer-fists, and palm strikes. Each has its advantages and drawbacks. Punches are fantastic; they have a solid and relatively small boney striking surface great for penetration, but an amateur puncher runs a high risk of breaking the metacarpal bones in the hand if the punch is done incorrectly (it's called a "boxers

---

[5] Don't misunderstand, the first thing you target when someone is running at you with a knife is *center mass*, and a lot of it. But because many bad guys nowadays wear body armor, the head and pelvic girdle shots are alternate ways to stop their advances if center mass isn't working.

fracture" for good reason). Palm strikes serve to protect the bones in the hand better and have a larger striking surface, which is good in some cases and not so good in others. Palm strikes have a shortened reach compared to punches by up to 2-to-3 inches. Hammer-fists are an amazing compromise between punches and palm strikes, are likely the most versatile strike with regard to angles, levels, and directions, and are actually the single most instinctive strike. Primates hit with hammer-fist strikes. Toddlers throw tantrums using hammer-fist strikes. You already know how to do it; it just needs a little refining to be more effective.

Other weapons include elbows, knees, shins, and the feet, and occasionally the head, though training is definitely needed to be able to effectively and safely deliver head-butts. We can't cover them all in this book, but let's break down the important ones.

Punches: Straight punches, as I said, are fantastic tools when you learn to use them correctly and safely. You can generate an immense amount of force with a straight punch, it's hard to see coming, and when landed well, it often knocks people out or disorients them.

Here comes our WTF: The straight punch is made with the fist closed, and contact occurs with the two largest knuckles (ironically the ones at the bottom of the Peace symbol). When making a fist, start with the smallest knuckles by taking your four fingertips (not the thumb) and them down onto themselves until they're tucked tightly into the palm. Now, fold the thumb down over the first two fingers. Squeeze all the air out of that structure. Air in the fist will allow the bones to move and collapse more on impact, possibly causing injury to your hand. Additionally, it acts as a shock absorber, which takes away energy from your punch. Imagine you have a small water-soaked tissue in your palm, and you're trying to wring out all the water from it. That's your fist. Of course, you'll tire out your arm if you keep it clenched the entire time, so just tighten it before impact.

The best places to target with a straight punch are the face, side of the face or jawline, or any other soft target, including the lower abdomen, groin, or neck. To deliver a good straight punch, the fist should come from the shoulder, jaw area on your body and unfold in a straight line to the target, never rotating your fist more than about 45 degrees inward. In other words, your fist should *not* be horizontal at the end of the punch; it should be about 45 degrees rotated in from the thumbs.

To get power from the punch, use the ground. We use what we call "kinetic linking" when striking, and it starts from the foot pushing on the ground to drive the leg slightly forward, which in turn links to the hip rotating forward in the direction of the strike, which in turn rotates the torso, and finally the rotating torso points the punching shoulder toward the target, maximizing the body weight behind the punch and dramatically increasing the mass that your two knuckles can deliver.

Palm Strikes: The weapon in this strike is the base, or heel, of the palm. That's the large area just above the wrist, about the bottom ¼ of the front of your hand. Leave the hand open, but position the fingers together to avoid them getting caught on clothing or body parts, potentially breaking them. It's usually most comfortable to have a slight bend in the fingers.

Targets for the palm strike are much the same as the punch, but you can use this on the side of the head as well as the back of the head with less chance of injury to your hand. The ear and base of the skull are great targets for the palm strike. The palm strike delivery is identical to that of the straight punch, but the 45-degree rotation inward is more critical here to protect the wrist on impact.

Hammer-fists: The hammer-fist is the bread and butter of hand self-defense strikes. This strike is the single most instinctive strike we humans have. If you ever call me and say, "I need a two-hour self-defense lesson because I'm backpacking across [insert continent] alone" (True story — thanks "master" for the one-and-done myth), I will make you wear a backpack and drag me around the building while you do hammer-fists and scream like the third monkey on Noah's ark for two straight hours. You won't like me very much for 24 hours after that, and hopefully you'll never have to thank me.

To deploy a hammer-fist, make your fist the same way you would for a punch. This time, though, the striking surface is the bottom of the fist, the part where the pinky finger is curled up. Keep in mind that you aren't actually hitting with the pinky finger, but rather that fat meaty part of your palm.

Targets here are pretty much any part of the body, but the face and head are best for stopping an attacker. However, when not standing upright or facing your attacker, you have many other options.

Because of the versatility of the hammer-fist, we categorize the strikes as forward, downward, and horizontal. Imagine you have an ice pick in your hand, the point facing down in your fist. Any direction and angle you can imagine stabbing something with that ice pick is a viable option for a hammer-fist strike. The main thing to remember is to use your body weight with every strike. That means *moving* your body in the direction the strike is traveling. A slight, downward weight drop should accompany a downward hammer-fist on impact. A sideways hammer-fist or one swinging horizontally should be accompanied by a rotation of the body. Think of how a baseball player rotates his body when swinging the bat, or a lumberjack when swinging an axe. It's the same motion.

Start with your elbows bent and make a good fist. Then, send the bottom of your fist toward the target, unbending your elbow and moving your weight in the direction of the strike along the way. Generating a lot of power in this strike requires good timing because you want your elbow to be about 80% straight and your weight to reach the apex at the same time your hammer-fist hits the target. Practicing this move is paramount.

Why is the elbow only 80% straightened on impact? As with all circular or arching strikes — as opposed to linear strikes like straight punches — one key factor in ensuring your body weight is transferred into the target is to make sure your elbow joint travels *past* the target. As far as the hammer-fist goes, think of your elbow as the last hinge on a jointed weapon before the business end. All your mass energy is going to be on or below that hinge. Imagine a hammer with a hinge in the middle of the handle. If you swing the hammer at a nail and stop the hinge above the nail, only the weight of the hammer's head will strike the nail because the hinge stops the hammer's mass. But if you swing past the nail, then the force you built with your arm and body also hits the nail through the hinge.

So as an example, using the hammer-fist, imagine you're delivering a blow sideways to the face of an attacker that's off your right shoulder around 90 degrees. When rotating into the side hammer-first technique, your elbow should travel past the attacker's face so when your fist strikes the face, your mass is transferred to a point past the target, therefore hitting the attacker rather that stopping at, or short of, him. Apply that physics lesson to all of your hammer-fists with the exception of a straight forward hammer-fist, which is a linear strike.

The hands are only 20% of your effective

"personal impact" weapons. Let's look at a few others that you should have in your toolbox.

Elbow Strikes: Elbow strikes are also quite versatile, like the hammer-fist, and can be absolutely devastating. Even accidental elbow strikes hurt people. Boxing matches are stopped because of accidental elbow strikes all the time, and cage type fights often end when one fighter gets to land several of them in a row. They are effective largely because of the large boney structure of the weapon, and the fact that the weapon has only one joint (hinge) that connects it to our body's mass, the shoulder.

Elbow strikes can also be thrown at multiple angles. In fact, they are so much like hammer-fists, that in our seminars we often train them in tandem because, for many angles, an elbow strike is simply a hammer-fist without un-bending your arm. This comparison and duality significantly cuts down training time to proficiency. Look for this same idea when I discuss knee strikes and kicks in the next section.

The striking surface for a forward or upward type elbow strike is actually about one inch out (toward your hand) from the tip of the elbow. For backward or downward strikes it's about two inches in from the tip (toward your shoulder). Although using the tip of the elbow works and can easily cut the thin skin on someone's face, we prefer to use larger, boned areas for impact. Remember, shutting down the brain is one way to stop someone, so we prefer "crushing" blows to "cutting" ones.

Targets for the elbow strikes are varied depending on the situation. Because you can use elbow strikes almost as effectively from the ground as standing, almost any part of the body that presents itself can be a target. However, if you're looking for stopping power, the head is your best bet. The top, or crown line and above, of the head is very hard, so you should almost never target that with any strike except perhaps a palm strike. And in any case, the head isn't always available for a strike. Then, the abdomen, groin, ribs, liver, and kidneys are all good targets to buy some space and do some damage. It depends on where you are in relation to these targets that will determine which one is best to use. I've even used elbow strikes to the legs before with a fair amount of success!

You can deliver elbow strikes horizontally in front of you, to the side, or behind you. You can also deliver them vertically behind you low, rising upward behind you, rising upward in front of you, and downward in front of you. These angles are mere guidelines; you can strike anywhere in between these seven basic angles.

To develop the elbow strike, again think about the hammer-fist and how you generate power for it, and employ that for the elbow strike. Keep your arm bent as much as possible throughout the entire strike, but particularly on impact! An unbent elbow will give a little bit on impact, acting as a shock absorber and taking energy out of the strike. You don't want that;

you want all the mass and energy to be transferred. Don't forget to move your body weight in the direction of the strike. Horizontal circular, angled strikes generally require you to *rotate* your body, whereas linear, vectored strikes usually require you to *shift* your weight. For either type of strike, remember that anyone that requires you to hit them with an elbow strike deserves to be hit with everything you have!

Regular Front Kick: This kick looks like what you probably picture in your head as a kick to the groin. In my experience as a trainer, I've found that most women can do this instinctively somehow. My wife, it seems, has some kind of super-human "testicle radar." I'm kidding — sort of. Because my wife is my business and training partner, I can honestly say that my wife has kicked me in the nuts more than any other husband in the world. If I'm wrong — seek help.

But all kidding aside, the regular front kick is often mistaken as a groin kick. In Krav Maga for instance, it's the poster child for no-rules self-defense training — a kick to the groin, which is against the rules in pretty much all sanctioned fighting sports. But any legitimate Krav Maga trainer will tell you that it shouldn't be considered just a groin kick. It's a perhaps better described as a kick to any relatively horizontal target.

The part of your leg that you should aim to use for contact (your weapon) is your shin. Not your foot, contrary to popular belief. The ankle is a joint with a ton of ligaments and can be prone to injury if hyper-flexed, and the foot has many small, vulnerable bones in it. This is probably not important if you are kicking the groin, but if you kick an attacker's head or knee, those small bones are going to hobble you. Using the shin bone gives you a harder, stronger weapon and is far less prone to injury. Not to mention it's a smaller surface area that will allow for more penetration on the target.

So, yes, targeting the groin is a good example. We also refer to it as the "A-frame" target because the insides of the legs also offer good targets (the femoral artery), and the follow through leads to the groin anyway. But if your attacker is bent over at the waist, the head or face may also be available and, for stopping power, a far more desirable target than the groin. Contrary to popular belief, groin kicks don't end fights — they start them. You may get lucky and land a great groin kick that doubles your attacker over in pain, but that's more of a movie scene than reality. Remember, stress and adrenaline are working for the bad guy too, and the pain of a groin strike will likely be delayed. So treat a groin strike as a distraction that gives you the ability to then attack the head or other vulnerable target with a higher stopping probability. For all intents and purposes, any horizontal target at your waist or below is a possible target for this kick. Even an outstretched arm could be targeted.

To deliver this kick, start by driving the knee up *and* forward simultaneously. To get your knee moving forward, you'll have to start driving your hips forward, and that's exactly what you want. Just make sure your hips don't initiate the movement, causing a "telegraph". Telegraphing is a term used in to describe a movement that can 'signal' or give away your intentions to your opponent, like winding up for a punch. Doing so gives your target a chance to move or defend your kick. As you do this, your knee should bend about 90 degrees. Take care that your foot never travels backwards, away from the target while doing this (think about the foot "trailing" the knee just slightly in the initial movement). As the knee approaches the target's height, viciously begin to un-bend your knee. Note that the knee never "holds" at the 90-degree angle at all. Rather, it hits that angle and begins un-bending right away.

Point the foot forward while un-bending your knee to extend your leg, expose the shin bone better, and to accentuate your hip drive forward. You should continue to drive your knee so that it *passes* the target height to ensure that your body weight is going through the target (the last hinge — sound familiar?). Because your hips are driving forward, the end effect might look like you're leaning backwards to the untrained eye. But we never lean away from the fight. The fact that your hips are both extended forward gives the illusion of bending backwards but, in reality, your upper body is still very much over and in homeostasis with your base leg.

Knee Strike: The relationship between the elbow strike and the hammer-fist juxtaposes nicely with the knee strike and regular front kick. There is little more to explain about the knee strike that isn't in the regular front kick description.

Of course, the weapon, or contact surface, changes from the shin to the top or front of the kneecap. And when delivering the knee strike, keep your leg bent (like the elbow strike) as tightly as possible. The purpose of maintaining this angle isn't as much about absorbing a shock, like the elbow strike, but more about making your leg harder to catch during the strike because there's less of an opening behind the knee to grab. It also strengthens and hardens the striking surface of the knee — like how squeezing all the water out of a tissue in your hand makes a stronger fist, the same is true for the structure of the knee.

Targeting for the knee strike is much the same as the regular front kick too. Believe me when I say that even a glancing knee strike to the head can solve a lot of problems. But the great thing about knee strikes is that they are also quite effective at targeting vertical surfaces. In fact, you will likely derive more power from your hips driving the knee forward than you will driving it upward. Again, almost nothing changes in the function of delivering a knee strike versus a regular front kick, with the exception of un-bending the leg. Keep it tight for the knee strike.

The beauty of the similarities of the regular font kick and the knee strike is that the only real split-second decision you will have to make is about the target's range. Assuming you are able to make a lower body strike at a vulnerable target, you can treat everything like a regular front kick, and simply not unbend your leg if the target moves closer, or you can think about it as always being a knee strike, that requires you to unbend your leg if the target moves away. Hick's Law has less of a foothold (pardon the pun) on you for this reason.

Although there are additional strikes that you should know and practice, I have overviewed the basics, which are most often used as the "simultaneous counterattack" to your defense of the immediate threat. It's not a coincidence that there are fewer leg techniques than upper body techniques. As humans, we need both our legs for balance and movement, particularly in the chaos of a violent altercation. Add to that the instinctiveness of using your hands and arms for defense and offense, and you can probably see why. There are other self-defense kicks that you should learn, but they require more practice than the knee strike and regular front kick to be effective. For example, a vertical target front kick (or 'Teep' kick in Muay Thai) is another staple of self-defense but requires an understanding of timing and distance that you can only get from training with a live partner in a dynamic setting.

Defenses:

I really stressed the fact that defenses should be as close to an instinctive reaction as possible: both to speed up the reaction time and to minimize the learning curve. But so far, I've only given specifics on offensive strikes, not defensive techniques. As I previously noted, this book isn't meant to be a full manual. If you're reading this book as the sole act of self-protection training, then read the hammer-fist section 100 times, tie 100lbs of weight to a sled and drag it around while throwing strikes to a pad that someone is holding while trying to tackle you. You're welcome. But, if you want a starting place to dig into some real tactics, what follows are a few general defenses for some common, unexpected attacks.

Haymaker punch defense: As far as instinctive reactions go, there is likely nothing more instinctive than raising your hands and arms up to cover your face when something hurls toward you. Just do an image search on the internet for "baseball bat flying into crowd" and you'll be rewarded with hundreds of examples of human instinctive reactions.

So, when caught by surprise and a haymaker punch is coming your way, you'd be hard pressed to do anything other than move your hands and arms up in front of your face and toward the threat. This isn't a perfect defense, but at least you're moving in the right direction. Let's refine this instinctive reaction to give you the best possible chance for success.

- As the arms move up, use the same side arm as the side that the attack is coming from (mirror image) to build your defense.

- Keep a 90-degree bend in your elbow. It's a strong angle for your arm, and it keeps the striking object furthest away from you without causing a sliding or redirecting effect on contact.
- Defend the attack, meeting it at 90-degrees. In other words, if the attack is perfectly horizontal, your forearm should be perfectly vertical on contact. If the punch is coming downwards at a 45-degree angle, such as a hammer-fist, then your forearm should be also at a 45-degree angle, creating a right angle against the attack.
- Try to make contact with the attacker's arm, wrist-to-wrist, keeping your hand open and fingers together (like a karate chop, except you're not using your hand).
- Move your body weight *into* the attack, be aggressive, and go get it. This will be the best way to sponsor your counterattack with body weight as well.
- Keep your eyes center mass of the attacker, not on the punch. You'll need to see everything that's going on and have a view of your target for your counterattack.
- Simultaneously with your defense, send a straight punch to the attacker's face!

Most likely, both your arms would have been moving instinctively in the first place, so these minor adjustments to a movement you already know makes learning quick and shortens, if not eliminates, perceptual lag. Your simultaneous counterattack hopefully resets the attacker enough so you can follow up with more strikes, or even better, disorient him enough for you to get away.

We call this the 360-degree defense, because you can use these principles to defend yourself from attacks coming from the outside in in a 360-degree vertical circle. Even if an attack is coming from down low and rising up toward your gut, you can still use these principles to make your defense and counter. If it is coming from that angle, it's probably a stab and not a punch. So now I'll discuss how to handle a stab.

Ice Pick Stab defense: Because trying to recognize the difference between a punch and a stab in the moment is futile, we treat punching and stabbing attacks the same. All the points in the haymaker punch defense apply to a stabbing defense. Even if the stab is coming upward instead of downward, the same principles apply. The only difference is what you might do *after* the initial defense is made. Note that once you understand the dangers involved, you'll want to start practicing using the same follow ups for both punches and stabbing attacks, simply because you're not likely to know which is which.

After the initial defense and counterattack (the hardest, fastest, most accurate best punch you've ever thrown in your life), you'll have two options: disengage or continue to try to control the attacker's knife arm and continue the counterattacks. However, you may not be in control over which one comes next. This is another reason that practice and training is so important. You *can* make split-second decisions based on the attacker's actions and reactions once your head is in the fight, but you *can't* get your head in the fight if you haven't trained on this scenario to become somewhat inoculated to it under stress. You *can* change your actions in fractions of a second based on the tactile sensitivity of feeling where your attacker is going, but you *can't* learn that from a book, video, or in a one-hour seminar. Because the selection of these follow ups require training and practice, we generally only include one follow up in our short seminars and a long speech about needing both options.

The first option for a follow up is to disengage and create space (because space = time) immediately after the strong counterattack. Your goal here is to create as much space as possible between you and the attacker, thereby buying time. A bonus is if you can deliver a vertical target kick or defensive front kick to move the attacker even further away while you're creating space. You might be using this time and space to access your own weapon, find one in the environment, find a shield, or to escape and evade. This option to disengage may happen either by choice or because of where the attacker went after the counter. Let me explain further.

If you feel a fantastic counterattack has landed, and the attacker stumbles, rolls his eyes, or otherwise has a dramatic reaction to the punch of your life, you may be better served to quickly exit if the option is available and get a few locked doors between you, or get in your car. Otherwise, you might use this time to arm yourself for a better defense. You may even *plan* to make a strong counter followed by a front kick to create enough space to draw your firearm if you're carrying one.

But you may have to disengage because of the circumstance. Imagine that your counterattack landed squarely, moving the attacker back a foot or two, but he is still very steady and in control. This would be a very, very bad time to stay in striking range or even close the distance. Once you lose contact with the attacking arm and the attacker creates a little distance, your chances of successfully defending another stab and landing another counter are lowered considerably. So, even though you were hoping to control the attacking arm, your window of opportunity has diminished. In this case, it is best to disengage and create more space, forcing the attacker to come back into your space if wants to attack again.

An alternative is for you to burst even further in and take control of the arm that's attacking you. This sounds like a dangerous prospect, but what part of this entire situation isn't dangerous? You either take action on your terms, or you leave your future entirely up to the attacker. But make no mistake, this is a high-risk situation, and you are connecting yourself to someone who has a knife. Practice, practice, practice.

To accomplish this alternative, once you make the initial defense and counterattack, your defending arm should stay up against the attacker's arm, such that you can drive it backwards with yours, moving your entire body so as not straighten your arm too soon. Once you've moved as far forward as possible, which hopefully forces the attacker's arm behind his own shoulder, you want to wrap up his upper arm tightly. Do this somewhere around the bicep or elbow joint by reaching over his arm, hooking around, and wrapping it up. This is known as an *over-hook*. The reason you should wrap the arm up that high is because the hand/wrist area is moving the fastest and has the most space. It's far easier to wrap around the bicep and then slide down to control more of the arm movement later.

Some of you may worry about the attacker's ability to still control his lower arm and cut you, but these cuts will be completely superficial and are very unlikely to cause serious damage. The reward for controlling the arm far outweighs the risk of minor cuts to your back.

However, this will be difficult to achieve safely if the attacker is moving backwards, in which case you would have to revisit the idea of disengaging. But assuming you landed a fantastic punch, momentarily stunning your attacker, the burst and control will serve you well.

Once you've controlled the attacker's arm, you need to do more damage. One thing you don't want to do is to get into a tug-of-war with the attacker. Who wins a tug of war? The bigger, stronger person. And you're likely at a disadvantage if you rely on sheer strength here. As previously explained in the principles of self-defense, you should continue counterattacks if given the opportunity to safely do so. When the attacker's knife-wielding arm is wrapped up, you'll want to keep your inside arm — the one closest to the attacker's center line — in a position to inhibit him from stepping around you. The most basic way to accomplish this is a "side" or "half" clinch. Your wrist and upper forearm will press against the attacker's neck, continuing down to your elbow and pressing onto his color bone and chest. Your hand will curve over the trapezius muscles and grab his skin, clothing, or whatever it can.

Now you have some control over the attacker's body, and your inside, or clinch, arm now acts as a barometer for you. A barometer measures pressure, and that's what your arm is doing. It'll tell you if the attacker is pressing forward, trying to get around you to get the knife back, lowering himself for a takedown attempt, or moving away from you. All the while, you are delivering vicious knee strikes to the groin or abdomen. You can also mix it up with elbow strikes to the face or head, but be careful not to give up the clinch position for too long. Make your elbow and go right back to it. Headbutts are also a possibility here — as are some kicks. Really the only rules here are: 1) don't let go of the wrapped arm, and 2) keep the side clinch position as sturdy as possible.

The 360 defense, burst in, and wrap control solution thwarts stabs or slashes that come from any angle. There are only really two small differences that you need to consider. First, when the attack comes from a low angle, bend at the waist to make the defense and go after it. Bending at the waist will keep your defense further from your body and defend the attack at an earlier time (bonus: it also puts your body weight into the defense). The second difference is the type of arm wrap you use to control the attacker; you would now go for what's known as an *under-hook*, in which your arm goes under theirs and wraps around it, the opposite direction of the over-hook!

Disarming an attacker with a knife is, for the most part, a fantasy hocus-pocus movie magic move. Drill this into your head: Your two options are to control the knife arm and do damage, or disengage and escape, arm yourself, find a shield, or re-set. Period.

---

6 Our in-person seminars do teach several simple disarms *after*, and only after, you've done a great deal of damage to the attacker. These require a lot of practice, but you do have one other option: break the arm. If you have a fully wrapped over-hook on the attacker's arm, and you've slid your hold down toward his wrist, you may be able to sharply rotate your whole body into the attacker and beyond (if you have their right arm wrapped with your left, then you are rotating right). This explosive rotation while you are holding the arm low near the wrist may break the wrist or hyper extend, if not break, the elbow. Either of those injuries will prevent further attack with that arm or hand. But it doesn't necessarily disarm the attacker, so this is still considered a combative move.

This description and the other self-defense techniques I describe in this book are not comprehensive lessons. To better prepare yourself, there are more comprehensive self-defense manuals, and I will be writing a follow up to this book that provides more detail. For now, find a place to train in your hometown.

The best way to disarm a knife attacker is to kick the knife out of his hand while he is unconscious.[6] Get it?

Handgun Threat Defenses: These are very high-risk situations. Just like in a knife attack, the risk is very high. But given no other choice, what will you do? Please understand that this section is a brief overview, think of it as a skeleton of principles that require additional techniques.

Gun threat defenses focus on an attacker's *threat*. If you have been paying attention, knife defenses are used against actual attacks, but here, we're talking about a gun *threat*. If a gun attack already started, you need to move and find cover. What I'm instead describing here is what to do *if* you decide you *need* to make a defense when someone is threatening you with a handgun, and they are within reach. You see this type of threat mostly in hold-ups, muggings, kidnapping, and sexual assault. But anytime a gunman wants to exert power over you by threatening to shoot will have a high probability that it will be in close range. Generally speaking, in these types of threats, the gunman wants something from you, not to just shoot you.

When caught by surprise, your instinctive reactions to a gun in your face may kick in very much like the reaction to a baseball bat flying at you in the stands — your hands go toward the threat. This is less likely if you had some kind of foreknowledge of the threat or were engaged with the attacker first, but anecdotal studies via CCTV footage of liquor and convenience store robberies show both the instinctive hands reaching and grabbing reaction, and the back off and don't be a threat reaction.[7]

Luckily, this instinctive reaction to reach for the threat lends right into the start of your actual defense. The principles of firearm threat defenses are:

1. Redirect the line of fire
2. Control the firearm and line of fire
3. Attack the gunman
4. If possible, disarm

Let's dive into each one a little more. This will also be important when we discuss third-party protection and taking down an active shooter.

In re-directing the line of fire, there are a few things to keep in mind. First, this is your initial movement in any gun defense so you'll want it to be as least detectable as possible. Keep in mind that you will be making an offensive movement toward the gun! If you're detected, you will alarm the gunman!

Right now you may be thinking: "No way, how can I possibly win this race?" You're not alone. Most people think that your redirecting movement has to beat the gunman's trigger pull, but this is not the case. In the end, what you're racing is the gunman's *recognition* of

---

[7] This is similar to a frightened reaction when people get smaller by shrinking away and lowering the head, and in this instance is often accompanied by raising the hands up, palms forward in a universal "I'm not a threat" body language movement.

your movement, a decision to act, and the act of pulling the trigger. In my 20 years of testing against someone who *knows* my intentions, I have yet to lose this race. How? I cheat. I cheat by using every advantage at my disposal. Here are the top things to remember when redirecting the line of fire:

- Move your hands first. The hands are some of the fastest things we can move on our body. (My wife would say my mouth, and that's probably true, for me!) The more of your body you move, the more likely the gunman is to recognize your movement. Keep your movements small and direct to the gun.
- Redirect the gun itself if at all possible. Trying to redirect the arm of the hand holding the gun may allow the gun to stay in its current position even for a fraction of a second, and when we are talking about firearms, we are talking about fractions of seconds. Take. Every. Advantage.
- If you believe the gunman wants something from you, it is likely that he is talking. Remember, multitasking is a myth. If he's talking, he can't simultaneously concentrate on something else. Attackers, like us, have to switch tasks. That takes time, and as long as you're subtle and quick, it's

more than enough time for you to redirect the weapon.

The second thing to keep in mind is that you aren't dealing with a mannequin. Once re-directed, the gunman's own instincts will be to put you back in the line of fire. It's a bad idea to redirect the gun's line of fire by striking it or batting it away. Most likely and most troublesome is that the attacker will pull the gun back toward himself in an instinctive retention movement. Try to grab something from a reluctant toddler, and you'll get the *"mine!"* reaction. They'll grab it with two hands and pull it.

To solve these problems before they happen, once you've redirected the line of fire, you must take some kind of control over it. For starters, whatever it is you do, *you must go in toward the gunman.* Remember, he is likely going to pull back on the weapon. If he doesn't, it's no big deal because now you're inside of the line of fire. But if you catch him by surprise, he will be.

There are only two ways I advocate for controlling the weapon after redirection: grabbing the gun or wrapping the arm. (Remember knife defense control? The wrap is the same). And bursting in toward the gunman while you perform either one is paramount. When grabbing, the gun will point back at you if you stay in place while the gunman pulls back on it. When wrapping, if you don't burst in, you may miss the arm altogether because the gunman is pulling it back.

Additionally, regardless of whether you're wrapping or grabbing, you need to counterattack simultaneously. We've already discussed counterattacks, so I will simply remind you that they are so important that they may be the deciding factor between success and failure; and failure can mean serious injury or death.

While you're bursting in to wrap, it's a good idea to use an elbow strike because a wrap will put you in closer to the gunman. If grabbing, punch them on the way in (a punch is a longer range weapon than the elbow, so it will get there sooner). I don't advocate a punch while wrapping because it will require you to stay a bit further away from the gunman, and in wrapping the arm, getting deep inside is very important.

When grabbing the gun during the redirection, you'll need to drive it toward the gunman as you move your feet toward him too. This will help you keep your weight on the gun, and move it in the direction that: 1) he's likely to be trying to move it to keep it away from you, and 2) takes away most of his ability to point it back toward you. Make that life-saving counterattack punch on the way in, and then *immediately* put two hands on the gun. One hand on the gun isn't enough for control. And even if the attacker only has one hand on the gun, he is holding the part that's meant to be held (the grip) and his own instincts will likely send his other hand to the gun now as well. The best way to control the line of fire on a handgun is with an over/under two-handed grip, mostly resembling the "Gable Grip," a common way to grip your hands together in wrestling. To see what I mean, clasp your hands with your palms together, offset at about 45 degrees, basically the way most people clap. Your thumbs form an X by crossing each other. Now, do the same thing, but keep your thumbs pressed against your pointer fingers on both hands. You'll be grabbing the thumb side of your palm on one hand with all five fingers, and the pinky side of your other palm with all five fingers. That's the Gable Grip. To translate that to controlling a pistol after making a redirection by moving the line of fire then grabbing the gun, imagine holding the gun by the barrel (around the forward part of the slide and forward frame, in front of the trigger guard on a semi-automatic pistol) with your thumb toward the muzzle with one hand. Send your other hand *under* the wrist of your first hand and grab the rear of the gun (back of the slide or hammer section). You now have a grip that closely resembles the Gable Grip but is separated by the length of the gun.

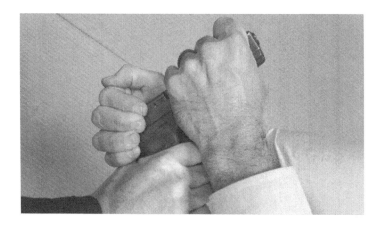

This grip gives you great control over the line of fire. Push and put your weight on the barrel side hand, and pull back slightly on the hammer side (or bottom hand) of the grip. Now, it's very difficult for the gunman to put you back into the line of fire. While this happens, you need to continuing striking with your knees or other leg strikes to keep the attacker occupied and off balance, physically and psychologically.

With firearms, you do have to consider that a disarm may be more important than with a knife for the simple reason that a firearm is a ranged weapon with penetrating ballistic ability, meaning that it can still be used against you while you are escaping or if you're behind a locked door or in a car. In other words, your options for avoiding and barricading are more limited.

In the example above when controlling the gun with both hands, a sharp rotation 90 degrees along the barrel's axis may loosen or even open the gunman's grip on the weapon, not to mention the help of your relentless strikes. Rotate the gun sharply and explosively on that axis, and then move the gun toward your side. *Do not move your feet yet.* If the attacker's grip isn't broken enough yet, you may end up pulling the muzzle back toward you and putting yourself back in the line of fire. Move *only* the gun first. If the gunman's hand is still on the gun, continue striking and try again when appropriate. If his hand is no longer on the gun when you move it to your side, then you can move your feet and begin to create space. Keep striking though, as the attacker is likely to attempt to re-acquire the gun. (This is where being good at the "fight" is important, and why reading or watching materials cannot replace physical training.)

What you do after you have the gun is entirely dependent on the situation. You may be able to simply get away at this point. Or, you may have to use the gun to defend yourself (or others) further, either as intended or as a blunt object. However, if you know nothing about guns, this would be a difficult time to learn. There's a good chance the gun malfunctioned while you were struggling for it, or perhaps it wasn't operable to begin with. If you are not familiar with clearing malfunctions or the operation of handguns, your only option is to use it as a bludgeon. Just keep that line of fire off yourself when using to strike someone, and again keep in mind he may be trying to re-acquire the gun. For this reason, don't go chasing after someone if he or she is running away.

Regardless of whether you appreciate guns, own guns, disapprove of guns, or outright hate guns, you should learn how they operate. There are over 300 million guns in the United States, and there's a good chance you're going to come across one at some point in your life. That doesn't mean you'll be assaulted with one, but you're likely to encounter one. There's also a good chance that you are next to someone that carries a gun almost any given day of your life.

If you're already familiar with gun operation, and you're not opposed to practice and physical activity, you should find a place that will train you in their use under *stress*. Accuracy with a firearm is hard enough, and under stress, it's an entirely different animal. Not to mention the skills involved in clearing a malfunction and doing so in the midst of conflict. You need to practice under these conditions if you intend to be able to perform at these times. *If you would like to attend one of our training seminars on firearms, from beginner to expert, visit* www.tacticalkm.com *for information on courses year-round. Our courses are built with this reality as their primary objective, not as an afterthought.*

As with everything we do, we attempt to keep defending yourself from a gun threat as simple as possible. If you get the chance to train with us or another reputable group, you'll find that we strive to train for all possible scenarios of threat, such as an attacker holding a gun in your back or lying on your back with an attacker on top of you. We train you on how to navigate these situations and provide as few options for immediate action as possible. We want you to react, not to overthink. In times of crisis, almost any action at all is often better than inaction. As Theodore Roosevelt once said, "In any moment of decision, the best thing you can do is the right thing. The worst thing you can do is nothing." Taken from the German philosopher Meister Eckhart's adage that the price for inaction is far greater than the cost of making a mistake. Even slightly flawed action can be adjusted on the fly, but no action puts you a long, long way behind the curve. Of course, as long as you've studied the principles in this book, run mental scenarios, and hopefully in the real world, and have practiced taking action, then your immediate response has a far better chance succeeding. Remember, self-defense is not rocket science, but it does require a realistic understanding of violence and a fair dose of physical practice.

Although I've provided a lot of information here about defending yourself from a gun threat, remember that this is not a manual. What this chapter attempts to do is to teach you important principles and give you tips on using every advantage possible. When searching for a place to learn and practice actual techniques, let these principles help you find reputable training. Not all "self-defense" lessons, courses, or schools are created equal, and the techniques are as varied as individuals' opinions on the subject. It's a profession ruled by ego, so keep an open mind, but question everything you're told and judge it against the realities of violence, not theory. You will not find a perfect solution because violence is always unpredictable, but you should be able to separate real trainers from snake-oil salesmen.

In Defense of Others. Action during mass casualty events.

It's sad, and it breaks my heart that there is no shortage of examples to choose from for this topic. The Oct 1, 2017 Las Vegas music festival mass murder happened during the editing and revisions of this book. It seems every time I'm preparing to give an important presentation or seminar, or write an article, another event takes place. A while back, we started using the hashtag #dosomething in conjunction with a multi-day, active shooter training course we were delivering at a State Patrol Academy for hundreds of people, both civilians and law enforcement, from all over the United States. That hashtag persists today, as I locate and share stories where average citizens stepped in and helped someone or helped end a situation instead of turning on their smartphones and recording the event. Nothing gets under my skin more than to see someone suffering, getting injured, or dying while other people record it. I could go on, but suffice it to say that if it's done in my presence, words will be, and have been, exchanged.

But it's not just the recording phenomenon that prevents people from helping. The "Bystander Effect" has obstructed rescues for decades. The Bystander Effect can be, and has been, the subject of entire books. It is a social-psychological phenomenon in which individuals are less likely to offer help to a victim when other people are present. Sometimes it's for fear of failure or injury, other times it's the thought that someone else will come forward to help, or that help is already on the way. I was in Las Vegas preparing for a large seminar at a national conference where I was teaching a group of about 100 martial artists how to intervene in an active stabbing attack on another person. A few days before my seminar, this happened:

> "(On July 4th) Police and a witness interviewed...said passengers trapped in the moving train huddled at both ends of the car and watched in horror as Spires (Attacker) punched 24-year-old Kevin Joseph Sutherland until he fell to the floor, then stabbed him until he was dead. Court documents say the victim was cut or stabbed 30 or 40 times, in the chest, abdomen, back, side and arms. Police said the assailant then threw the victim's cellphone and returned to stomp on Sutherland's body."

The Washington Post; July 7, 2015

Here, Spires, tried to rob the victim of his iPhone. What's important to us in this section is that there were a dozen other people in this single train car.

"I was waiting for someone else to step in, then I would've helped out. There's nothing I could have done on my own," said one witness. "We were in a moving train," said another. "You're not really sure what you need to do... This man is holding a bloody knife. I don't think anyone was going to try and stop him."

I do not judge the folks on this train. No one, except police officers, is expected to intervene in situations that have this level of violence. There is no shame in staying out of harm's way and staying alive or unhurt. Many of these witnesses became victims as well because the attacker turned to them after the murder and demanded money. No one else was injured, and everyone complied (notably, this is how terrorists get people to comply as well: start with brutality and note that no one else will get hurt if...). Who can blame these victims? They just witnessed a brutal, physical attack by a mad man. Any one unarmed (important point here) person would have a serious problem confronting this attacker.

But look at that first witness quote again: "I was waiting for someone else to step in..." This is a vitally important thing to realize when we talk about intervening in violence: the importance of someone taking leadership.

On September 11, 2001, United Airlines flight 93, one of the hijacked planes, likely headed for Washington to kill thousands more, was the scene of the ultimate #dosomething. A group of passengers, after hearing what happened to the other hijacked planes, knowing that they were all going to die, decided that they had to do something. "Let's Roll" became the battle cry of millions of Americans against terrorism that day. Thousands of lives were saved, and our nation was spared even greater chaos by the possible decapitation of our government and destruction at our capital. All of that was spared because someone, likely several people, became leaders that morning in the face of overwhelming odds.

One of my favorite videos on active shooter or mass casualty violence interventions that shows the importance of being a leader, even if sometimes inadvertently, is the security camera footage from a bus. A man in the back of the bus is standing up, and pulls a gun from his waistband, and robs a seated passenger nearby. Another passenger in the back sees this, is visibly alarmed, and stands up and approaches the mugger from behind, ostensibly to do something. The mugger moves forward, pointing his gun at another unsuspecting passenger and robs them. [8]

---

[8] Before I continue, it's important to note here that almost all the passengers had a level of situational awareness somewhere around zero (except for our would-be hero), and most had their faces and attention buried in their cell phones.

At the scene of the second robbery, our would-be hero looks like he's about to do something, then stops as the robber moves forward to continue. Clearly, he had all the intention of doing something, but you could tell from his body language that he didn't know what to do.[9] (Which is why training and practice is important, folks!)

The mugger makes his way forward on the bus, and sticks his gun in the face of yet another seated passenger, who is buried in his iPhone *and* has ear-buds in. What happens next is a textbook case study. First, the unsuspecting victim looks up, sees the gun, and has a fearful, instinctive reaction to grab and redirect the gun from his face, almost exactly as we described in the last section! Although he had no formal training, it was a reaction to do something in the face of danger.

Here's where it gets cool: This victim now has become the unwitting leader of a movement. As soon as he made his instinctive defense, and added control by pushing the gun into the mugger's stomach as he stands up (I swear this guy has been to one of my classes before!), our would-be hero now had the opportunity he

[9]The mugger was completely oblivious to the fact that a fellow passenger was following him the entire time, within only a foot or two! Tunnel vision under stress happens both ways — for the good guys and the bad guys. If you want to mitigate the effects of stress, you have to undergo stress inoculation training, which is training on the very scenarios that will ultimately cause you stress. The bad guys get better at it every time they commit crimes without getting caught.

wanted, and a partner to help him, making up for the skill he lacked! He then jumped into the fray to help take the gunman down, as did several others that were just robbed or took notice. As other passengers scrambled to get out of the way, third and fourth heroes wrestled for the gun, held the mugger down, struck him, and — most entertainingly — our latest victim was wrapping his ear-buds cable around the mugger's neck in an attempt to strangle him! What a great example of an *improvised weapon in the environment — YAY!*

There you have it, once a leader stepped up and started the movement, more people were able to jump in, feeling like they had help, and were less likely to suffer any consequences alone. Our training seminars incorporate teaching people what to say and how to say it to get others to help. Becoming the best leader you can in a time of crisis also means being able to actively and intentionally lead other people. In many cases, people will follow the leader, but think about how much more effective you would be if you knew how to bark orders and delegate to other people to solve problems! You'd be a superhero leader — that's what you'd be!

You have learned your first lesson in third-party defense in this video: You will be most successful if you have three things: skill, opportunity, and partners. We refer to this as the SOP of active threat mitigation. SOP is cool because it also stands for standard operating procedure because we want this formula to be just that for you, your family, and your personnel — a standard procedure you can employ when deciding how to act against violence.

I'm going to work backwards through our acronym here, because skill will take the most explanation.

Partners: Having friends is a wonderful thing. Having friends when you have to fight for your life is a must. While you can take down someone actively shooting or stabbing, you will likely need more skill than just the study of this book, a ton of bravado, a warrior's mindset, and a super healthy dose of luck. It's better if you have some help.

Without going into too much detail here, it's very, very difficult to fight or defend yourself against more than one person at a time, and it's *nothing* like the movies. Unfortunately the media have given most people a false sense of hope, that if they just train enough or workout enough, they stand a chance taking on a whole gang of bag guys. Nothing could be further from the truth. Fighting more than one person at a time requires a ton of movement, massive amounts of skill, amazing tactics, and most likely a few weapons. Even then, the odds are, literally, stacked against you. So with that being said, stack the odds in your favor by making sure you have some help when you're ready to confront evil.

If you decide to be a leader and #dosomething, you'll want to be confident and order other people to help. *Don't ask for help, tell them exactly what you want them to do.* You can do amazing things against a knife-wielding attacker with just two people and a couple of chairs. It's more than likely people want to help, but they don't know how. Be the expert, or at least act like you play one on TV. Formulate a plan, tell people what they are to do, and make it happen.

Be careful not to overcomplicate your action. When taking down an armed active threat, you want to have at least one partner, preferably two. Three is possible if you have an open area, but four or more will be too many in most cases. Extra people will only get in your way.

In my days working in nightclubs, and as an audio engineer in concert venues, as well as decades of working with various law enforcement agencies, I can tell you from experience that it is way easier to take someone down with one other trained partner than it is with five people pulling in opposite directions. Inevitably, some people trying to help end up working against the direction you're trying to go, and if you pull someone in multiple directions, you tend to actually stabilize them. It's like when you watch a running back from your favorite football team run up the middle and into a bunch of defenders while his own offensive line is pushing him forward. Usually, the ball carrier ends up stuck in a standing position and in much of a stalemate when the ref blows the whistle.

The maximum number of people you want to take down and disarm one attacker is four including you, the leader. You will be in charge of the weapon arm because you're reading this book. The others will be on the attacker's other arm, the legs (one person), and the head if you have a fourth available. If you're only working with three people, the head gets skipped. If it's just you and a partner, you're on the weapon arm and upper body, and your partner covers both legs. Further detail will be provided in the skills section. After you takedown and disarm the attacker, if you want more people for restraint, be my guest. Just make sure they're doing something useful.

In a section I wrote for the Practical Aviation Security textbook regarding in-flight defense against a threat for airline crews, I discussed the limitations of the environment they would be working in, and how they'll likely only have room for one partner in the initial takedown. The idea was for the takedown to happen on the deck of the aircraft, and not sideways into and onto other passengers in the seats, possibly complicating the issue if the bad guy would slip down to the deck inside of a row of seats, limiting the crew's ability to control his arms. The same is going to apply for any limited space you may encounter, like a theater or concert venue. Communicate that to your partners and try to control the direction of action.

Your partner may not be another individual. In the absence of any living help, arming yourself can help move the odds window in your favor. A living partner will help do damage or control an attacker. A weapon can help disable, confuse, or stun him, also achieving damage or some level of control. Best-case scenario is that you will have a weapon *and* friends, but be sure you've trained yourself on using the weapon, so as not to become a liability to your living partners. This includes pepper spray. Pepper spray can easily affect your ability to help or hurt efforts to control the attacker. I can't tell you how many stories I've been told of police officers getting sprayed by — you guessed it — their partners.

Opportunity: You have to choose the right time to act. An opportunity must present itself or you risk becoming part of the problem. Running in the open, straight toward a firing gunman is not your best opportunity for success. In another video that I use for training, a student stopped a shooter at Seattle Pacific University in 2014. One person was killed, and two others were wounded when the shooter entered a dorm hall from outside where three other students were. Another student, armed with pepper spray, stayed just out of sight around a pillar, and as the shooter attempted to reload his shotgun, our hero in shorts, a t-shirt and no shoes, sprung into action, first spraying the shooter in the face, then tackling him, and taking his shotgun away. The hero then ran back around the pillar, removing the shotgun from the equation, and came back just as the shooter pulled out a hunting knife from his belt. Our hero then slammed into him again and threw the knife out of reach, holding the attacker down until help arrived.

The right opportunity presented itself at that moment for him to act, saving lives. He didn't have to engage; he could have escaped down the hall and out the back, but he decided he had to do something and did it well, even without partners. Though in this case, his pepper spray took the place of a live partner, which most weapons can do. If you have to go it alone, having a weapon to help disable, confuse, or stun the killer is a good replacement.

Just recently in Illinois, math teacher Angela McQueen rushed a shooter from behind as he was spraying the high school cafeteria with rounds. In my own state of Colorado, David Benke tackled a 32-year-old gunman who was open firing on kids in a middle school parking lot (two kids were shot and survived, but David prevented more shots from being fired).[10] Both these teachers and the student I mentioned in SPU had an opportunity and took it. After the initial action, partners did show up to help in all three accounts. Some of those partners just needed a leader to take action before they joined in.

Skills: In the three incidents mentioned above, our heroes didn't necessarily have any special skills or training in taking down active shooters. But they all had some training of some kind: Our student hero at SPU was a hall monitor and a student security guard. Some limited training probably existed and more importantly, he surely felt that it was his *duty* to do something. Angela McQueen was said to have just gone through some kind of active-shooter training, most

---

[10] Side note: what the f*ck is wrong with people?!

likely not instilling any real skills but certainly giving her the confidence and drive to take action. David Benke is a big guy and a college basketball player. He was accustomed to physical contact, most likely in the context of highly competitive collegiate sports, and at least somewhat used to aggressive behavior. Each of these heroes used whatever skills they had to bring attacks to an end.

Most mass shootings end with a gunman suicide upon being confronted by authorities. The latest massacre at the Las Vegas concert was no different. But often, the response time of armed authorities is precious minutes. Police simply cannot be omnipresent. We have a saying we use often in our seminars, "When seconds count, police are only minutes away." In fact, in an FBI study of mass shootings from 2000-2013, 40% of shooters committed suicide, most when they felt that they would be stopped. Twenty-eight percent engaged in gunfire with the police, 13.1% were safely and successfully stopped and restrained by civilians, and 3.1% were stopped by armed citizens. Alarmingly, more than half of all active shooter incidents were over before the police even arrived, which on average took only three minutes. Seconds count, my friends!

Below are some skills to practice to better your odds at successfully becoming your own first responder, or "immediate responder" as we prefer to call it. Again, this is an outline of physical skills you should take and practice and improve, under the supervision of a professional. When you are running toward a murderous individual with no regard for life, yours is on the line.

Active Shooter: Like most of this book, this section assumes you are unarmed. If you plan on being a concealed firearm carrier, please make sure you are properly trained in the access, use, and protection of that firearm. If you decide to carry a gun and can't keep someone from taking it from you in a fight, you are a liability to society, not an asset. You'll find more information on this and the entire subject in The Modern Gunfighter.

Once a shooting has begun, if you've made the decision to act but you're unarmed, you need to close the distance between you and the gunman. In a perfect world, you'll be able to utilize cover to get close and approach from behind. I'm super sorry to break this to you, but the world's not perfect. You'll be lucky to have any cover to leap-frog in.

Assemble your partners quickly and have them fall in behind you. This next part is imperative: Assign them jobs. Keep these tasks super simple. Let them know that you are going in front and will be grabbing the shooter's arms and the gun. Your partners need to be right behind you, and the number-two partner is responsible for the legs. Quickly show this person how to wrap up someone's legs to immobilize them. Here's how:

Shoot in low at knee height so your head is no higher than the attacker's hamstrings, or just somewhere between the knee and the hips. Hit his legs *hard* from behind or the side (most damage from the side) with your shoulder as you wrap your arms around their upper legs. Grab onto your own arms at the crook of the elbows if you can reach them, or at least your forearms to lock in that "bear-hug" of his legs. *Important*: continue to drive through his legs so that he will fall (as long as you have his legs hugged tight, he can't step for balance). As he's going down, wrap *your* legs around his lower legs and stick the front of your ankle/lower shin behind the knee of your other leg and fold that other leg down tight. This creates a "figure 4 lock" with your legs around his. Keep your head pressed in tight to his legs and hold on. You now have your entire body stuck to his legs to essentially immobilize him.

You should quickly explain this before you go in, but you can always bark commands in the moment after you have the gunman on the ground.

Remember, as the person going for the gun, you are now responsible for keeping your partners safe. Keep talking to them throughout the encounter and give commands or updates as needed. If you have a third partner, you can direct that person to help on either the legs or the arms and gun, or directly ask that person to strike the gunman's head, hoping for unconsciousness. You'll be able to feel when your second partner has good control of the legs because the gunman will be struggling hard but not moving at all. Immobilizing the legs makes all the difference!

Let's rewind a bit. Back to your approach, do your best to approach rapidly and unseen. If you can close the distance from behind, that's best, but really anywhere from the shooter's 4-o'clock to 8-o'clock positions will do. The hope is that he'll be so focused on what he's doing in front of him, he will not notice your approach. The sound of gunfire will mask the sounds of your approach, as long as you're not screaming your battle cry on the way in. But whatever you do: move fast, be decisive.

When you get to the shooter, approach from the side that's firing the gun. For illustration purposes, we'll say the gunman is right handed, so you are going to approach from his rear-right. Keep low when doing this next part, so that your head is at shoulder height or below, masking your reach from their vision when you pass them. Without touching the gunman, reach forward with your outside hand (the one furthest from the gunman, in this case it would be your right hand) alongside his outstretched arm toward the handgun or the barrel and make first contact there. *Grab* the barrel or slide of the gun for leverage. Like the principles of self-defense against a gun threat, the goal is to immediately affect a redirection of the line of fire on first contact. You may not be able to stop them from shooting everyone, but you can stop them from shooting the next someone so *move* the gun while grabbing it.

Next, you'll use your inside arm, the one closest to the gunman, in this case your left arm, and come from *under* his arm or arms, wrapping everything up tight and hugging it all to your body. If it's a long gun involved, instead of wrapping under his arms, you can wrap over his arms for more leverage, or even just grab the rear of the gun on the stock somewhere. When doing this, you're going to want to "put on the breaks" and move your body weight back toward him. In other words, you were moving forward in the direction the gunman was shooting, once you redirect and wrap, then move back toward him so that everything is crushed between your bodies.

At this time, your partner should be hitting his legs hard. Clench your teeth because you're going for a ride. Your goal is to stay as *close* to the gunman all the way down to the ground and smother him when you get there. As you're going down, you can use your feet for leverage and make sure you end up on *top* of the gunman. If you end up on the side, you'll be fine, just work your way up to a straddling position and keep your weight on him. Be careful not to kick your partner in the head as you step over to straddle. Keep those arms wrapped up tight and maintain a tight grip on the gun so he can't move it around and do more damage or point it at your partner.

If you don't have a third partner, now is a good time to start barking orders to anyone else around that can help. You need to put this guy out of business fast, but you and your partner are a little busy at the moment. If you can't get someone to step up and start stomping on this guy's head, you'll need to find a way to do it yourself. Head-butts and elbow strikes will be your first line of weapons, because you don't want to let go with your hands. If you get a couple of good strikes off and can separate the attacker from the weapon, do it. You can then use the weapon as a bludgeon.

Once you've taken control of the weapon, and the gunman is no longer struggling, and assuming he is the only threat, use improvised restraints to bind the ankles and wrists. Be sure to bind the wrists behind the gunman's back, not in front. At this point, you *don't* want to be walking around holding the weapon. The situation is hot, and the police will be arriving and expecting a life-threatening altercation, and you don't want to be mistaken for one of the bad guys. *Do not hold the gun.* Secure the weapons out of anyone's reach and keep an eye on them. Your new job is as a medic. You may carry a tourniquet or two with you and maybe even an Israeli Bandage. Care for the wounded as best you can and direct others to do the same and wait for authorities. You've done well.

Active Stabbing: If I'm being honest, I'd rather deal with a gunman than an active stabbing. Knives are harder to control because you can't grab them; therefore, you can't use the same leverage you can when you grab a gun. In addition, the knife is dangerous from *all* angles. The gun is only dangerous from one.

However, there is one glaring advantage you have intervening in a stabbing versus a shooting — safety offered by distance. A firearm can harm you from some distance; a knife cannot cause injury outside of a few inches. So the *real* solution to intervening in an active stabbing situation is to find a blunt object nearby and swing for the fences, aiming for the attacker's head. Some examples are a fire extinguisher, a drawer from a filing cabinet, a bat, a stout briefcase, or your shin bone (if the attacker is on the ground).

There is another video we use for training that takes place in Rotterdam, Holland, on a public sidewalk in broad daylight. The attacker is seen seated, straddling his victim (his ex-girlfriend) and stabbing her repeatedly. It's a fairly gruesome video, and we only use it in high-level training sessions. I'll put you at ease right now and tell you that she did survive after being stabbed over 70 times in and around the neck and face.

The reason we use this video is not for the perspective of the victim, but to take a look at the witnesses and others around. Aside from someone recording the event, you do eventually see two and then three bystanders try to help. The first two repeatedly try kicking the attacker, mostly "push" kicks, all to the body, and none of them are successful. In fact, the attacker is actually so focused on his violence that he barely notices them or their efforts at all. Every time I watch that video I scream at the screen, "Kick him in the f*ckin' head already!" Remember, shut the brain down!

It's only after someone pulls the attacker off by

the hood of his jacket that the violence stops. You see three attempts to pull him by the hood; the first two are unsuccessful, and the attacker doubles his stabbing efforts on his victim each time.

I don't blame the would-be heroes for not ending the incident sooner; in fact I applaud them for doing anything at all, and likely saving her life in the process. Heroes for sure, they put themselves at risk. But I do wish that someone had trained them, even just a little, on how to be more effective. A swift kick with your shin bone to the attacker's face or side of the head surely would have ended the attack sooner. While I don't recommend it, if you want to see the video, it's available freely on the internet. Just search "crazy Dutch man stabs girlfriend."

So when faced with having to intervene against a knife attack, use your environment and improvised weapons. If none are available, and the attacker is standing so you can't get a good shin-to-the-face kick, you may decide to grab some partners and go hands on.

All the prep work that I discussed earlier also applies to intervening in an active stabbing incident. Same set up, same partners, same approach. The difference will come in how you, the lead person, will control the knife arm. There are three different ways to do this, but two of them require just enough timing and talent to be relegated to "you need more training for this." So I'll lay down one simple strategy.

Make your approach the same as it was with an

active shooter. Approach from the rear-side that wields the knife. Now you're going to do almost the *exact same thing* on first contact, but instead of grabbing the knife as if it were the gun (it'll be moving *way* too fast) you're going to want to wrap over the attacker's stabbing arm with your lead arm (your right arm if you're approaching on the attacker's right) somewhere around their elbow or upper forearm, and wrap under his upper arm with your inside arm. If you reverse those and go under/over instead, you'll probably still be ok. Just like with the gun defenses, you want to put the brakes on and crush back into the attacker, hugging that arm like your life depends on it (it just might). About this time, your partner should be hitting and collecting those legs, and down you all go.

Your ability to deliver good strikes on your own is going to be much, much harder than if the attacker had a gun, because you need to control the arm and minimize damage from the knife — a difficult task under the best of conditions. If there's blood, that arm will get very slippery. Be practiced and comfortable with head-butts, because those will be your best option for strikes in the moment.

There is one very nasty detail left: The attacker's other hand is still free, and you don't have any kind of hold on the knife itself! This allows the attacker to switch hands and use the knife in his left hand against you and your partner. Having three or four heroes in this situation helps a lot.

But if it's just two of you, you need to be delivering devastating strikes with your head and maybe your knees, and at the same time trying to isolate the knife from the reach of his other hand. There is simply no way to discuss all the variables involved in this action in this book. These types of situations require time on the mat in a legitimate, reality-based, self-defense training center. If you are familiar with some grappling terms and techniques, you might try to work to an armbar to break the arm, or to a figure 4 (kimura) hold to tear the shoulder up. Again, these take practice.

Out of the three ways we have to intervene in an active stabbing, this one offers the least control and does the least amount of damage to the attacker initially. But it is by far the easiest to learn in a short amount of time. I wrote several "how to" articles on this subject for Black Belt Magazine that you may want to look up for some of the other, more favorable options. But remember, nothing beats being armed with something to shut the attacker down quickly.

Becoming a superhero: Your plan of action after this book

I hope you are never in a situation that requires you to know any of this. But people who have been in these circumstances probably didn't think it would be them. This stuff happens, and if it happens in your presence, I hope you saw it coming and tried to avoid it. If you couldn't, I hope you have the confidence and skill to find an opportunity, identify some partners, and take action.

After reading this book, I hope you remember to pay closer attention to the world, and people, around you. Become a student of body language and non-verbal communication. Develop a plan of action for the areas where you spend a lot of time: work, school, home, restaurants, theaters, and shopping malls. Talk to your kids about what to do in an emergency, and practice the plan. Take a training course on emergency first aid. Put together a kit that you carry all the time with a couple of tourniquets and Israeli bandages. Remember, you might be the one that needs those things, not just other people! Blood loss can cause death quickly. Keeping as much of the red stuff in the body as possible until medical help arrives is important.

In short, take control of your AAA violence insurance. Be Aware, practice Avoidance, and learn how to take Action. Start getting into better physical shape and conditioning level than you are now, whatever your ability level. Running away is physically demanding. Running away fast is even harder. Fighting is harder still. Remember, strong, healthy people are harder to kill and are generally more useful.

How can you learn more about taking action? Locate a self-defense school or instructor and start practicing some of the life-saving techniques I described here. Nothing can replace hands-on instruction. There are many places that teach self-defense, some legit and others not so much. Here are a few things to keep in mind when looking for physical training for yourself, loved ones, employees, or a group:

- Make sure the school or instructor teaches stand up striking, ground techniques, and techniques against weapons. I'm biased, but Krav Maga is probably the best balance of all three right now. Not all Krav Maga is created equal though. There is no legal protection for the name so you may find Krav Maga in your neck of the woods, but it may not be actual Krav Maga training. Do your homework.

- The training should include stress training and scenario training. Learning movements in a sterile environment or without practice under stress is like learning them from a book. You won't be able to access these skills under real stresses that come from real violence.

- *This one is important:* Any physical training techniques and practice methods should assume you don't know what attack, if any, is coming, or when, and you are caught by surprise. If the self-defense techniques only work when you're "ready," they won't help you in real life. Practice should always include "free work" where you have to defend against any number of things without knowing what is coming, and it should all be done while you're under some sort of simulated physiological stress.

- You don't have to be in good shape to start learning, but a good self-defense program will include fitness activities and will get you into shape *while* you're learning. You should be working up a sweat when training; this isn't scrapbooking.

- Generally speaking, making grown adults wear white pajamas to learn self-defense is kind of ridiculous. (A martial arts uniform or 'gi' pronounced gee, is usually white and looks like bad pajamas. See Karate Kid for reference.) Some systems like Brazilian Jiujitsu, a great grappling and ground fighting system, is built around wearing the uniform, and the gi is actually used in some techniques, particularly in the sport form of the art. That's okay, as long as you understand its use. The same goes for Judo. But most true self-defense training centers will encourage attire more akin to a gym.

- Watch some classes. Do simulated attacks look real or do they look static, without much movement or follow-up. Take knife defenses for example. Is the attacker stabbing and then leaving his arm out there like a statue so his partner can perform a series of moves? That's unrealistic. Stabs are dynamic and repeating, and the attacks should look like that.

- Lastly, make sure the instructor or institution has been teaching the advertised system for a while. For instance, Krav Maga schools where the instructor has only been training in Krav

124

Maga for a month are popping up all over now. We're seeing a lot of Karate schools advertise "Krav Maga Adult Self Defense" with little-to-no background in actual Krav Maga training. Sure they may have 20 years of Karate experience, but that's not reality-based self-defense. Just like if you're looking for Karate or Kung Fu, don't go to a Krav Maga school! Again, do a little homework.

If you would like more advice on where to train in your city, contact me through our website www.wetrainsuperheros.com, and I'll try to point you in the right direction. I've been teaching self-defense for 20 years and have worked all over the world, since before reality-based self-defense training was even a term. I know most of the reputable organizations out there, as well as the less-than-reputable ones.

Lastly, reach out to us at the same website if you'd like us to come to your school or business and help you develop a plan of action, talk to your employees or group, or set up a series of training seminars. We've already helped dozens and dozens of corporations and companies large and small, as well as colleges, charter schools, churches, and city and county government employees get trained and develop a plan of action. We'd love to help create a safer community in your neck of the woods, too!

Good luck in your training, and thank you for taking the time to learn how to combat evil in this world, because it starts in your own community. Make your workplace a safer environment just by being in it. Be an asset in an emergency, not a liability. And most of all, go forth and be awesome every day!

ABOUT THE AUTHOR

James Hiromasa grew up in Hawaii where he worked in nightclubs for the better part of 10 years, before moving to Colorado and working another decade in the concert industry.

Beginning his study of martial arts (Judo first) at age 9, there has rarely been a time that James didn't practice one martial art or another, including Taekwondo, Hapkido, Kickboxing, and Krav Maga. He currently holds several black belt ranks including 3rd Degree in the Israeli Self Defense System of Krav Maga. James was in the very first group of instructors to be licensed to teach Krav Maga in the U.S. in 1997 and was one of the first 2 in the U.S. outside of the National Training Center to earn an instructor's black belt. James was also on the Krav Maga Advisory Board and, at the time, was one of only a handful of instructors to hold "Train the Trainer" status, meaning he was qualified to train and certify instructors in the highest levels of Krav Maga and has personally certified hundreds of instructors worldwide.

On an international level, he was among the first few ever to be awarded Senior Krav Maga Instructor status from the Wingate Institute in Israel. James most recently co-developed a comprehensive integrated firearms training program for law enforcement and civilians through the Tactical Training division of Colorado Krav Maga, and created the ACT Program (Armed Civilian Training) with co-developer, SWAT Firearms Instructor and fellow author Michael Miller (The Modern Gunfighter).

James is the CEO and Co-Founder (along with his wife Shannon) of Colorado Krav Maga, Inc., considered by many to be among some of the most prestigious and successful Krav Maga Self-Defense Training Centers in the country. In this role, James spends most of his time training instructors, working as a contract trainer for various law enforcement agencies, teaching seminars, and giving presentations in across the USA.

James has spoken to hundreds of employees, executives, and groups across the U.S. on Safety, Awareness, and Personal Protection and still actively presents to all types of industries and organizations. To book James for a presentation or training for your group anywhere in the world, visit www.wetrainsuperheros.com and fill out the information form.

Made in United States
Orlando, FL
28 March 2022